THE
FUTURE WORLD
OF
AGRICULTURE

Walt Disney World
EPCOT Center Book

THE
FUTURE WORLD
OF
AGRICULTURE

By Wendy Murphy
and the Editors of Grolier

GROLIER

Grolier Incorporated
President and Chairman of the Board Robert B. Clarke

STAFF FOR THIS BOOK
Editor in Chief Kenneth W. Leish
Senior Editor Bernard M. Garfinkel
Art Director Don Longabucco
Picture Editors Laurie Platt Winfrey
  Diane Raines Ward
Copy Editors Anne Glusker
  Lois Krieger
Editorial Assistant Susan Stellingwerf
Production Manager Valerie Plue
Assistant Production Manager Margaret Fina
Consultant Environmental Research Laboratory of
  the University of Arizona

COVER: Looking to the day when food will be produced in space, scientists in The Land grow lettuce in a huge spinning drum. The revolving motion provides a substitute force for gravity.

TITLE PAGE: Using new agricultural methods, Israeli farmers have turned desert into productive farmland.

Library of Congress Cataloging in Publication Data

Murphy, Wendy B.
  The future world of agriculture.

  At head of title: Walt Disney World EPCOT Center book.
  Based on the Land exhibit at Walt Disney's EPCOT Center.
  Includes index.
  Summary: Traces the history of agriculture with emphasis on future methods of farming and growing food.
  1. Agricultural innovations—Juvenile literature. 2. Agriculture—History—Juvenile literature. 3. Agricultural innovations—Exhibitions—Juvenile literature. 5. Agricultural exhibitions—Florida—Juvenile literature. 6. EPCOT (Fla.)]—Juvenile literature. [1. Agricultural innovations. 2. Agriculture—History. 3. Agricultural exhibitions—Florida. 4. EPCOT (Fla.)]
I. Grolier Incorporated. II. Title.
S494.5.I5M87 1984   630   84-12807
ISBN 0-7172-8142-6

ACKNOWLEDGMENTS

The editors gratefully acknowledge the assistance of the following: A. D. Brunson, Vice-President and Director, The Land, Kraft, Inc.; Dr. Henry Robitaille, Agricultural Manager, The Land; Carl Hodges, Dr. Merle Jensen, Wayne Collins, Environmental Research Laboratory of the University of Arizona; Dr. Joseph A. Angelo, Jr., Chairman, Space Technology Program, Florida Institute of Technology.

PICTURE CREDITS

The editors would like to express particular appreciation to the United States Department of Agriculture, Michael Melford and Wheeler Pictures for the creative photography at EPCOT Center, and Cooper West/Nicolas Enterprises of London for the artwork that appears on pages 10–11, 12, 98–99, and 109. The illustrators include Tom Stimpson, Lionel Jeans, Andy Farmer, Mike Saunders, Chris Forsey, and Geoff Taylor. Cover: Mitchell Funk. Page 2: Richard Novitz/Black Star 5: Library of Congress 6: Hank Morgan/Photo Researchers 8: Environmental Research Laboratory (ERL) 13: T K Rose, courtesy New York Botanical Garden 15: Charlton Photos. Chapter 2: all pictures by Michael Melford/Wheeler Pictures except for pages 18 top, 22 top, 25 bottom, 27 top 28: Walt Disney Productions 24, 31 left: ERL 20: courtesy Mitchell Beazley Ltd. and Random House, Inc. 32: Metropolitan Museum of Art 34: Musée de l'homme, Paris 35: Kongelige Bibliotek, Copenhagen 37: British Museum, London 38: Metropolitan Museum of Art 39: Brian Brake/Photo Researchers 40: Metropolitan Museum of Art 42: Arto Resource/Scala 43: British Library 44: Library of Congress 46: Granger Collection 47: top, Library of Congress, Thomas Jefferson Memorial Foundation; center left, John Deere and Co.; center right, McCormick Agricultural Library; bottom, Academic American Encyclopedia 48: Private Collection 51: Chicago Historical Society 52: State of Illinois, Department of Conservation 53: National Gallery of Art 54: Library of Congress 55: top, Bettmann Archive; center, Nebraska State Historical Society; bottom, Library of Congress 56: State Historical Society of Wisconsin 57: top, Library of Congress; bottom, New York Historical Society 58: Henry Ford Museum 59: top, United States Department of Agriculture (USDA), Research Information Staff; bottom, New York Public Library 60: top, Can Manufacturer's Institute; center, Kansas Historical Society; bottom, H. J. Heinz Co. 61: Wyoming State Historical Department 62: Runk/Schoenberger for Grant Heilman 64: Mitchell Funk 65: Michael Melford/Wheeler Pictures 66: left, Library of Congress; right, New York Public Library 67: Burpee Seed Co. 68: Academic American Encyclopedia 71: left, Wide World Photos/AP; right, ERL 72, 73: USDA 74: Stephen Brown/Wheeler Pictures 75: Runk/Schoenberger for Grant Heilman 76: top, USDA; bottom, DNAP Plant Technology Corp. 77: DNAP Plant Technology Corp. 78: Valmont Industries 79: top, Paolo Koch/Photo Researchers; bottom, Lee Battiaglia/Photo Researchers 80: Hank Morgan 81: Merle Jensen/ERL 82: top, Richard Novitz/Black Star; bottom, INCO Ltd. 84: top, ERL; bottom left, Hank Morgan; right, ERL 85: top left and right, ERL; bottom, Mitchell Funk 86: top, Lester Sloan/Woodfin Camp; bottom, Chuck O'Rear/Woodfin Camp 88, 89: USDA, Research Information Staff 90: top, Thomas Hopker/Woodfin Camp; bottom, Susan McCartney/Photo Researchers 93: left, USDA; right, Runk/Schoenberger for Grant Heilman 94: NASA 96: Boeing 97, 101: NASA 103: top left, NASA; right and bottom, USDA, Research Information Staff 105: Robert McCall 107: Merle Jensen/ERL

Contents

Apple picking in 1910

CHAPTER 1

The Future World of Farming: A Preview

Picture the farmer of one hundred years from now. Discard the image of a sun-baked tractor driver with grime under his fingernails and mud caking his boots. In the future world of agriculture, technical expertise, scientific knowledge, and computerized, robotic equipment may be far more important than the hard work and muscle power that farming traditionally required.

As he runs his elaborately engineered agricultural kingdom, the future farmer may have a lot more in common with white-coated chemists and computer-operating systems engineers than with the Farmer Browns of yesterday. He will supervise his farm from an office by punching a computer, spending far less time in the fields than farmers of today. His farm of the future will be an electronic one, automated and computerized, a marvel of agricultural science and technology.

On some of these farms, remote-controlled machinery will prepare the soil, plant the crops, then check and see that they get enough water and fertilizer. As the crops grow, other machines will wipe out any pests or diseases that threaten them, then gather in the harvest and send it off to market in a dazzling display of automated efficiency.

Fertilizers and pesticides will still be important in cultivating crops. But farmers of the future will be able to tailor their crops in dozens of ways by using sophisticated chemicals called "growth regulators." These chemicals will control how the crops grow—taller, shorter, faster, or slower, according to the farmer's needs. Dairymen, ranchers, and poultrymen will also use chemicals like these to manage animal herds, control their growth, and even regulate their moods. (*See Glossary, Plant Growth Regulators.*)

Most farmers will continue to grow grains and other staple crops. But in many cases, the farms they grow them on will be huge spreads or agribusinesses run like large industries. Even in less

Hydroponic lettuce, grown in nutrient-enriched water without soil, thrives in the controlled environment of an indoor farm in Connecticut.

7

developed parts of the world, the small farms of today will have to become bigger and more efficient to succeed.

Large industrial farms invest enormous sums of money in labor-saving equipment—machines that pick tomatoes, for instance. But an automated tomato picker can be used only for picking tomatoes, not for different kinds of crops. This will reinforce the trend toward monoculture, or single-crop farming. The waste that occurs today on many single-crop farms will be reduced greatly, however. About 20 percent of some crops are now passed over by automated picking machines and

left to rot during the harvest. New, fine-tuned equipment will correct this inefficiency.

Supplementing large-scale outdoor farms will be a new kind of farming, done indoors and known as "soilless" farming. It will concentrate on growing profitable and fragile produce, such as salad greens, mushrooms, tomatoes, strawberries, and garden peas, in laboratorylike settings with controlled environments. Temperature, air, sunlight, humidity, feeding, and pests all will be precisely regulated to create a kind of agricultural Garden of Eden. As for soil, there won't be any. Crops will be grown in sterile, or germ-free, sand or in water or even suspended in the air. Large crops of fish will be raised in aquaculture laboratories run in much the same way. (*See Glossary, Soilless Farming, Aquaculture, Controlled Environment Agriculture.*)

In the greenhouse below, in Abu Dhabi on the Persian Gulf, seawater from which the salt has been removed is used to grow vegetables in desert sand.

In some places, immense "biospheres," greenhouses in which the climate is carefully controlled and bad weather does not exist, will be built to house these new industries. Even now, experimental greenhouses, used to grow large amounts of garden vegetables, are operating successfully in different parts of the world. A number of these greenhouses have been built in coastal desert regions, for example, at Abu Dhabi in the Persian Gulf, and at Puerto Penasco in the Mexican state of Sonora.

Abandoned old factory buildings and obsolescent skyscrapers in the middle of crowded cities may also be converted into greenhouses. In the future, thousands of people may shop in these high-rise gardens. They will be able to buy fresh strawberries, tomatoes, and other foods just minutes after they have been picked.

Eventually, even amateur gardeners will use the techniques of soilless farming and aquaculture, creating a controlled environment in their own homes—in a family sunroom, for example. They will grow vegetables without using soil and raise other foods, such as fish, at home. The one drawback in all of these advanced techniques is that the food they produce may cost more than food produced in conventional ways.

Farmers who live on land that is not suited to large-scale farming, and those who still choose to run one-family farms, will use "closed-system" farming. Closed-system farmers will not raise one or two crops on hundreds of acres. Instead, they'll grow a variety of crops on fairly small-size farms. (*See Glossary, Closed System Farming.*)

This sounds like traditional farming of the kind practiced for two centuries or more by most American farmers, who raised cereal grains or cattle and at the same time kept a vegetable garden, a few chickens, a pig or two, perhaps some sheep, and grew fruit in an orchard besides.

But traditional farming wasted time and energy, as well as valuable resources that were difficult to replace. For example, farmers traditionally used massive amounts of petrochemicals (chemicals derived from petroleum), as fertilizers and pesticides. In contrast, closed-system farming is designed to waste very little. It will use few inorganic,

or man-made, fertilizers and pesticides, and it will provide for the long-term health of the environment. In closed-system farming, the farmer will scientifically select and manage each crop that is grown. Such a crop will not only make a profit for the farmer, but do many other things as well. It will be designed to keep the soil healthy, nourish a neighboring plant, make a troublesome pest harmless, feed a fishpond, fatten a hungry pig, and even fuel a tractor.

Agricultural futurists also forecast remarkable changes in the kind of land that will be used for farming. Until recently, experts believed that there was a limited amount of land in the world available for farming. Some, in fact, maintained that this amount was decreasing. The problems of used-up soil, limited supplies of water, and harsh climates will remain troublesome, of course. But today's new technological advances may permit the cultivation of millions of additional acres now thought of as unsuitable for farming. This land may have soil that is too salty or too alkaline. It may be hillslopes where the soil is eroding, carried away by wind and water. Or it may be land that has lost its fertile topsoil, hot dry deserts where little rain falls, or swamps clogged with water. In the future, all of these lands will be made to bloom with food crops through the skilled use of new farming techniques.

Providing More Food

There will be another important change in the future world of agriculture: the development of plants and animals that grow much better and

---

OVERLEAF: The farmer in this artist's conception of a farm of the future sits in his computer room (right), studying images of his fields beamed down from a small Landsat satellite. The red spots on the screen indicate crop stress that needs to be corrected. With the aid of his computer, which processes the data and suggests a solution, the farmer solves the problem. Robots in the field (one is seen at far left) take the corrective action ordered by the farmer. At center, the farmer's wife and child talk to the operator of a huge farm machine used for plowing and planting.

provide far more nutrition. Improvements of this kind will come mainly through breeding programs, which are among the newest and most exciting in all of applied science. New techniques of breeding will produce plants that are better able to withstand disease, drought, frost, and salty soil; plants whose fruits or vegetables all ripen at once and are ready for harvest in a shorter time; plants that make more efficient use of the sun's rays, grow larger and juicier, and have sweeter pods or seeds or leaves. The first such plants are already being readied for commercial use. Geneticists, scientists who study genes, which control heredity, are also working on new breeding programs for animals. They have already begun to develop

cows that provide more milk, beef cattle whose meat contains more protein and less fat, and pigs that will provide more pork.

Improving familiar foods is only part of the new program. Another aim is to develop entirely new sources of food. There are around eighty thousand edible plants in the world. Yet only about three thousand—less than 4 percent—are eaten by people around the world. Amazingly, of these,

In this fruit farm of the future, robots harvest oranges from trees that grow not in soil but in water-filled channels. Other crops are grown under domes that conserve available moisture.

just three cereals—wheat, rice, and corn—supply more than half of all the calories and protein that people consume. Another two dozen or so cereals account for an additional 45 percent. Plant scientists and nutritionists believe there are many new and important food sources waiting to be developed. These plants may radically change the diets of future generations, just as the discovery of the American potato and tomato changed the European diet three hundred years ago.

One such plant is the tarwi. This hardy and adaptable plant grows in South America's Andean highlands and produces pea-size black-and-white seeds that are high in protein. If the plant were grown in agriculturally poor parts of Asia and Africa, it could be a major source of protein and cooking oil. The West African miracle fruit is another candidate. Its sweet berries could become a future alternative to cane sugar. A third is the naranjilla, a golden South American fruit that tastes like a cross between a pineapple and a strawberry. There are numerous other promising new plants that could well become commercial crops.

The Coming Agricultural Revolution

In short, as we shall see, the future world of agriculture promises to produce a new agricultural revolution that will outpace the remarkable progress of the past. Consider how far we have come already. In ancient Egypt in the year 3000 B.C., a farmer worked his plot of land with a crude wooden scratch plow. His plot might be one-half to one acre of irrigated land. Over the course of a year he grew enough grain or garden vegetables to feed perhaps five people in all.

Four thousand years later in medieval England, a small farmer worked the land with a primitive horse-drawn plow. He might turn over and seed four to five acres. Over a year he harvested enough food for his family and two to three others.

By 1875, a typical farmer in the United States worked his land with the help of horses and new horse-drawn machinery, including plows, cultivators, harvesters, and threshers. He plowed 140 acres and in a year he fed his own family and sent to market enough grain and other food to feed between five and six other people.

Dense hair makes the naranjilla, which grows in South America, look inedible (lower right), but underneath is a richly flavored fruit. In the future it may be widely cultivated as a food source.

One hundred years later, agricultural productivity, the amount of food grown per acre, has risen dramatically. Today, the typical American farmer owns or rents 435 acres. American farmers make use of $111 billion worth of machinery. They plant the best seeds scientists have developed. With all this help, the typical American farmer raises enough food to provide an entire year's food supply for fifty people.

This book will trace some of the key events and important discoveries that have made this amazing growth possible. We will see how changes in farming have also changed our way of life, our surroundings, the kinds of foods we eat.

We will then take a close look at some of the exciting new developments forecast for the next century. By the year 2025 the world population may have doubled. Somehow farmers will have to feed twice the number of people they do today. The new agricultural revolution will make it possible for them to do so.

Some of the most promising futuristic scientific developments are already in evidence at The Land, the exhibit presented by Kraft at EPCOT Center in Walt Disney World. Within ten or twenty years, most of these advances will be a routine part of modern scientific farming. Other exciting ideas and experiments are now being researched and tested, and scientists are convinced that many of them will become an everyday reality. They have good reason for their optimism. A new era in scientific farming is under way, and it will change the shape of agriculture.

New Kinds of Foods

Future advances in agricultural technology will be paralleled by advances in the food-processing and chemical industries. Already, in little over a century, the food-processing industry has invented such techniques as canning, sterilization, dehydration, quick-freezing, freeze-drying, cold storage, controlled-atmosphere storage, and irradiation. They are now all routine ways of getting fragile produce from farm to market without spoiling.

Progress in this area will continue. In the future there will be a boom in the production of solid dairy foods such as cheese that do not need to be refrigerated. Various dried meats and vegetables that keep for many months on store shelves will be developed.

To make these foods taste fresh again, a cook will simply add water. And numerous new artificial foods—for example, artificial bacon and eggs—will be engineered to accomplish specific health goals, such as lowering cholesterol. (Cholesterol is a food substance that most nutritionists believe increases the likelihood of heart disease.)

An even more intriguing area of invention may be the fabrication of edible foods from such seemingly inedible or indigestible materials as cottonseed, maple and tobacco leaves, thistles, newsprint, coal, earthworms, and algae. In fact, scientists can mine just about any substance for its chemicals in order to design and manufacture entirely new kinds of food. (*See Glossary, Food Analogs.*)

For this purpose, farms may be joined with chemical factories. At one end, inedible plant matter will be taken in as raw material. It will then undergo a chemical process that reduces its proteins, fats, and carbohydrates to basic molecules, such as carbon, hydrogen, oxygen, and nitrogen. Finally, like pigments being mixed to make different-colored paints, these molecules will be reassembled into thousands of different artificial foods. The end results will be just as nutritious, if not more so, than the naturally grown foods we eat today. While most of us will prefer to continue eating natural foods, artificial foods could be used to prevent starvation and to supplement the diets of people in the less developed areas of the world.

One scientist who believes this will happen is Dr. Cyril A. Ponnamperuma, Director of the Laboratory of Chemical Evolution at the University of Maryland at College Park. "If we can make the material for our shirts in the chemistry laboratory," says Dr. Ponnamperuma, "why not the substance of our lunches?"

Whatever these foods may taste like, there is no technical reason why chemical foods cannot be produced right now. This is just one more example of the unusual solutions scientists are working on to expand food production.

Meanwhile, farmers around the world face more immediate challenges. They have to raise the most nutritious crops and animals possible. They have to do so without poisoning and spoiling the environment and at a cost that makes the food available to everyone. To this task they bring an adventurous spirit and ten thousand years of practical experience and know-how. For the future, they will have the help of the remarkable advances we will be describing in this book.

This lush Wisconsin dairy farm symbolizes the productivity of American agriculture. Alfalfa and corn grow in strips plowed along the natural contours of the land, preventing water loss and erosion of soil.

CHAPTER 2

Exploring The Land at EPCOT Center

Like a giant silver-and-glass crown, The Land exhibit at EPCOT Center towers over the great garden of exotic plants that surrounds it. Presented by Kraft, The Land covers six acres and is the largest exhibit at EPCOT Center. It is a unique educational and entertainment facility that provides visitors with a close-up, firsthand view of plants and aquatic animals being cultivated. Its purpose is to highlight, in a stimulating yet sound way, current ideas on food, food production, land use, and farming. In doing so, it demonstrates how an intelligent and constructive use of land can contribute to the future development of agriculture and, thus, to the well-being of the world's people.

A good part of The Land consists of a series of enormous greenhouses. This allows guests to visit the experimental growing areas regardless of the weather outside. The exhibit also contains two theaters and two restaurants, where the food served emphasizes the concepts of good nutrition.

Perhaps the most intriguing aspect of The Land is its greenhouses. Beneath their protective transparent roofs lies a whole new world of farming, in which crops grow winter and summer in tropical and desert environments, under controlled conditions.

New Ways to Meet Future Food Needs

The Land reminds visitors that, no matter where people live or what they do, they must have food to survive. And it provides an exciting showcase for advanced techniques scientists are experimenting with as they seek creative and imaginative ways to meet the food needs of the future, including a population that may double by the

---

In the Creative Greenhouse at The Land exhibit, lettuce grows in triangular boxes (left). Inside the boxes, water is sprayed directly on the plants' roots. At right, halophytes (salt-tolerant plants) grow in saltwater inside column pots.

The Land, presented by Kraft, Inc., welcomes visitors night (top) and day. Set on six acres, it is surrounded by gardens of ornamental, exotic plants.

year 2025. For example, The Land's scientists grow tomato plants without soil on conveyor belts that expose their dangling roots to nutrient-laden water baths. They raise fish and other aquatic creatures in transparent tubes where temperature, food, and waste removal are carefully monitored. And they cultivate lettuce in huge drums that spin constantly to provide a substitute force for the earth's gravity. This is one possible way of growing food on a spacecraft in a twenty-first-century space community.

More than thirty specialists in agricultural science are involved in the experimental agriculture at The Land. The project director is Henry A. Robitaille, a noted research horticulturist. The team includes agronomists, aquaculturists (specialists in the science of growing crops in water), and plant pathologists and entomologists (specialists in plant diseases and insects, respectively).

Some of the technologies displayed at The Land are also studied at one of America's leading centers for agricultural research, the Environmental Research Laboratory (ERL) at the University of Arizona. Established in 1963 under the direction of Carl Hodges, the ERL is dedicated to exploring new ways to improve agricultural production. It has pioneered numerous advances in agricultural science and technology, including the development of "controlled environment agriculture" (CEA), and has designed and supervised the construction of some of the largest and most successful CEA greenhouses in the world. The laboratory has also conducted research into scientific farming methods for the National Aeronautics and Space Administration (NASA) and the U.S. Department of Agriculture (USDA). The Land's team of scientists interacts with the ERL and with agricultural experiment stations, international research centers, the USDA, and numerous other organizations concerned with advanced agricultural research in order to insure that The Land remains on the frontiers of agricultural knowledge and development.

Seeing a New World of Agriculture

Visitors to The Land can see this new world of agriculture at three main exhibits. "Listen to the Land" is a thirteen-minute guided boat ride that gives twenty-three hundred visitors an hour a broad-based look at farming and food production, past, present, and future. They experience the challenges farmers face in growing crops in harsh climates and poor soils. And they ride through growing areas where ingenious and creative techniques are being used to grow crops that are vital to the world's food supply, as well as various plants that may become important crops in future years. They also see demonstrations of new agricultural

technologies that may find important uses in the future world of agriculture.

The Land's second exhibit, the Kitchen Kabaret, presents a humorous, entertaining, and informative song-and-dance show about healthy eating habits. Here computer-controlled *Audio-Animatronics*™ figures present an A-to-Z revue of nutrition. Among the colorful characters are Connie Corn, Mairzy Oats, Miss Ice Cream, and "the star of the show," Bonnie Appetit, a "nice wholesome housewife." Moving and talking in an amazingly lifelike way, the figures present numerous wise rules for developing a lifetime of good eating habits.

Symbiosis, a remarkable eighteen-minute motion picture, is the third main exhibit at The Land. *Symbiosis* shows how much people depend on their surroundings to survive. As the scenes in *Symbiosis* range over the entire globe, the audience sees how all things on earth coexist in an intricate chain of life. One of the motion picture's special concerns is with technological progress and how it can preserve or ruin the delicate balance of nature. The audience sees many examples of the ingenious ways people around the world have met the challenge of their environments. The

Visitors to the Farmers Market at The Land have a choice of eight food booths and enjoy their meals sitting beneath bright-colored, simulated balloons representing three of the four main food groups.

beautiful images and poetic narration of *Symbiosis* lead the viewer to a central theme—in the future, as in the past, agricultural progress must be based on a "creative partnership between man and nature," as the late scientist-philosopher René Dubos expressed it. *(See Glossary, Symbiosis.)*

The boat ride is probably the ideal way for visitors to begin their exploration of The Land. As it sets out on its trip through a tunnellike waterway, the audience gets a close-up look at the typical seed-grown plant beginning its life cycle in the earth.

How a Plant Grows

Whether it is a cucumber vine or a weed, a plant is a complex living organism. Like its companions in the animal kingdom, it breathes, grows, eats, drinks, reproduces, and eventually dies. Heredity, or the genes it inherits from its parent plant, determines many things about its life. Genes determine

The color of soil varies according to the climatic conditions under which it was formed and its composition. Shown above are the dark soil of cold tundra regions (1), light-colored desert soil (2), the humus-rich soil of semiarid grasslands (3 and 4), and the iron-rich red soil of tropical grasslands (5). The forest soils of cool, humid climates range from brown to gray (6, 7, 8, and 9).

what it will look like and what kind of seeds or fruits it will bear. But a plant depends on the outside world to supply its day-to-day needs, such as sunlight, carbon dioxide, water, and nutrients.

Sunlight is the ultimate source of all life on earth, and it provides plants with the energy to produce food. All other living things depend on plants for their energy. We get energy from plants in two ways: first by eating plants directly, and second by eating animals that have fed on plants. Sunlight, or solar radiation, provides heat, necessary to all chemical processes. Sunlight also triggers many of the plants' responses to its environment and its growth cycle. By the intensity of its light and the length of the days, the sun signals to a plant when to blossom and produce fruit.

From the soil, plants receive nourishment, water, and a certain amount of air. Soil provides a plant with a firm footing, a place where its supporting roots can take hold and grow. Soil also contains minerals that nourish a plant. It provides

plants with water and a certain amount of air. Soils are commonly divided into four broad groups: clay, silt, sand, and loam. Loam is the most fertile and has features of clay, silt, and sand all in one. Whenever there is a choice, it is used for most farming.

Water is a plant's third major need. An increase or decrease in the supply of water will often change the look of a plant in just a few minutes. This is true because water keeps a plant standing erect through the pressure it exerts on each of the plant's cells. Water provides a way for nutrients to travel from the soil to a plant's tissues. Water is the substance in which most of the chemical reactions the plant experiences take place—for example, the budding of new plant cells and the manufacture of natural growth hormones. Finally, water provides hydrogen, one of the essential raw materials a plant needs to build its tissues.

The life cycle of a plant starts with a dry seed that has not yet begun to grow. Within the seed lies all the information the plant will need to grow to maturity. Germination, or the growth of the new plant, begins when water penetrates the seed's outer coating and reaches inside to the live embryo, that is, the beginning form of the plant. Often germination requires a special combination of temperature and light, which is triggered by the start of spring. Some seeds respond early in the season, others much later.

Once the embryo is awakened, it starts to swell. It gets this first burst of energy by tapping its own food stores. Eventually the organism bursts through the seed case. Now the seedling pushes its tiny roots outward into the soil to anchor itself. It begins to gather up water and nutrients through thousands of tiny hairlike root tubes called capillaries. After a certain period, the plant sprouts upward. As it unfurls its main leaves to the sun, it becomes independent of its own food reserves. Then the plant draws most of its energy for growth directly from the sun by way of its many leaves.

Within each leaf lies the green coloring matter called chlorophyll. It is the vital ingredient in the important process known as photosynthesis, the process that makes it possible for a plant to make its own food. During photosynthesis a plant uses sunlight, air, and water to make starches, sugars, and proteins. Complex structures within the leaves work at this task like millions of tiny food factories, converting inorganic compounds in the soil and air into the food the plant needs to grow. *(See Glossary, Photosynthesis.)*

Each kind of plant has its own special needs, which must be met if it is to survive and prosper. A plant needs so many inches of water at certain stages of growth, so many hours of sunlight, so many days of temperatures above or below a certain level. It needs soil that is acid or neutral or alkaline—and so on. It is the sum total of these needs that makes each kind of plant suited to one kind of environment and not to another.

A Trip through the Greenhouses

A plant's surroundings, the physical environment it grows in, are a key factor in its growth. Different environments affect the kinds of farming that have been and are now being practiced in different parts of the world. To illustrate this, the "Listen to the Land" journey moves on to visit briefly three of the main climate zones that have challenged man from the very beginnings of farming. They are the tropical rain forest, or jungle, the desert, and the prairie.

As the boat enters the tropical rain forest, monkeys chatter and birds chirp. Plants seem to burst suddenly into life as rain drenches the thick and tangled vegetation. Tropical rain forests generally lie along the equator, where it is hot and humid all year long and where there is never much difference in the length of a day. One hundred to four hundred inches of rain may fall in a single year, depending on the particular location. Native plants in a tropical rain forest usually have large leaves. The leaves collect and evaporate excess moisture and are more successful in capturing the sunlight that filters down through the forest's thick canopy of tall trees. Some plants rise skyward on climbing vines—another way of obtaining sunlight.

The constant rainfall in the tropical area dissolves and drains away most of the earth's mineral nutrients. These nutrients are an important aspect of a soil's fertility, that is, how well crops will grow in it. Fertility is also affected by how acid or alka-line the soil is. Tropical rains, which wash away topsoil and mineral nutrients, create thin, acid, mostly sticky clay soil. When these clay soils are farmed, they become sterile or lifeless within a very few hours. The farmer must then abandon his hard-won piece of earth and cultivate another.

As the boat moves on into another climate zone, visitors see a quite different but equally harsh environment for farming—the desert, where endless vistas of sand are burned by a blazing sun.

Here the problem is not too much rain, but too little. Deserts may get less than ten inches a year. The soil, which is pure sand in many areas, rapidly absorbs this rainfall. In addition, desert air is extremely dry. Daytime temperatures often rise to well over 100 degrees Fahrenheit. The sunlight is harsh and glaring. The little moisture that is produced by nighttime condensation quickly evaporates in the hot daytime sun.

There are other problems in a desert. The temperature drops as much as 60 degrees at night, and there are frequent violent windstorms. It is little wonder that few things grow in the desert.

On The Land boat ride, visitors pass through experimental greenhouses. Onboard guides point out the innovative techniques being used.

The plants that do manage to survive are mainly a class of plants called xerophytes. These plants have various ways of coping with extremely dry conditions. Many of them, such as the cactuses, have virtually no leaves, because leaves evaporate moisture. The plants have other ways of conserving for themselves what little moisture there is. They generally are small in size, which means they

Hard work turned the seemingly inhospitable American prairie (left) into a region of prosperous farms (below), as these scenes from the "Listen to the Land" boat ride at EPCOT Center illustrate.

need less water. Their skin is thick, to protect against water loss. And their extensive root systems grow at a shallow depth and reach out far to get every possible drop of water.

Leaving the desert, the boat enters a third climate zone, the American prairie. As the narrator of "Listen to the Land" notes, the first settlers on the prairie faced harsh conditions, making it seem almost as forbidding an environment as the rain forests and the deserts. The settlers found the prairie covered by tough, six-foot-high grass whose roots reached down four inches into the topsoil. The soil itself was heavy and hard to work. Prairie fires started by lightning sometimes set the grass aflame. There were other hazards as well: storms, tornadoes, blizzards, and swarming locusts that devoured everything in their path.

Yet prairies or grasslands are a natural midstation between tropic and desert climates. They offer sufficient moisture for various kinds of grasses, but too little for trees. The American prairie, the Argentine pampas, the great plains of Hungary, the steppes of the Ukraine, the high veldt of South Africa, and the plains of Manchuria are all grasslands, and all are prime agricultural regions. They offer a combination of virtually level terrain, a temperate climate, a long growing season, moderate year-round rainfall, and loamy soils that are unsurpassed for fertility in any other zone.

In the United States, prairie farmers overcame the hazards they faced. They prepared the soil for farming and made the region this country's agricultural heartland, where corn, winter wheat, oats, barley, soybeans, and forage crops are raised and a substantial share of the nation's livestock are readied for market.

Aided by all manner of mechanized equipment, prairie farmers evolved what most Americans now think of as the typical American family farm. As the "Listen to the Land" boat proceeds on its journey, visitors see a realistic recreation of this midwestern farm, complete with family dog, barnyard pigs, and a crowing rooster. Gliding past the farm, the boat enters a theaterlike barn where visitors take in a quick-flashing display of photographs, film clips, and animated vignettes that evoke the history and development of the family farm.

Perhaps the strongest theme to emerge from this display is that the family farm is becoming more and more dependent on large-scale mechanized equipment. Along with scientific advances, such as better seeds, this has led to more efficient farms that grow more food per acre.

The progress of farming has been remarkable over the past one hundred years. But it has been directed at making farmlands in prairie and woodland zones more productive. Now efforts must be made to develop the untapped agricultural potential of the tropics and the desert. As the "Listen to the Land" boat moves into the huge experimental greenhouses, visitors can see firsthand how science and technology may make this possible.

The greenhouses are divided into three distinct workshops. The first reproduces a typical tropical environment. Here crops are grown that are important to the people of Southeast Asia, Africa, Latin America, and the southern United States. The peach palm, the winged bean, and the cocoa yam are three tropical crops not yet known to most Americans, but destined for wider use in the future. Varieties of bananas, pineapples, papaya, corn, sugarcane, rice, mung beans, and pigeon

In The Land, jumbo squash plants are intercropped with smaller vegetables. Trickle-drip irrigation provides moisture, and sticky ribbons control pests.

Amaranth grows with very little moisture, and its seeds can be made into a nutritious flour.

peas are among the dozens of other rotating plant exhibits likely to be on view and under test here.

In the Tropical Greenhouse, scientists grow more food in less space by using a method called intercropping, that is, planting one crop along with others. Corn and beans may be grown together, for instance. Corn provides vertical support for the beans, greatly increasing their exposure to light and therefore their yield. The beans, in turn, take nitrogen from the air and make it available to the soil and to the corn roots. In this way, intercropping provides a way to fertilize the soil naturally. *(See Glossary, Intercropping, Multiple Cropping.)*

The second greenhouse area is devoted to crops that can be grown in desert and semidesert areas. Here, as well as elsewhere at The Land exhibit, the staff continuously changes crops to test various plants and growing techniques. One new grain that has been grown in the Desert Greenhouse is triticale, which was created by crossing wheat with rye. Triticale grows well in poorer soils and it produces a high yield. (See "Hybrids and the Green Revolution," page 71.) Another new grain grown in the desert environment has been amaranth, a plant that requires very little water. Its abundant seeds can be milled into flour.

Two plants that may have a use other than providing food have also been grown in the Desert Greenhouse. A hardy plant called guayule produces natural rubber. And the *Euphorbia latyris* is a leading candidate for the production of fuels for transportation. We may someday make gasoline from it.

An advanced system provides precise control of irrigation and fertilization. Small plastic tubes buried in the sand carry carefully measured amounts of water and nutrients to each plant.

The controlled environment of the Desert Greenhouse makes it possible to achieve high yields of high-value crops. Lettuce and spinach are cultivated on polystyrene boards floating in a foot of water, for instance. Vine crops, such as tomatoes, melons, cucumbers, and banana squash, grow vertically by climbing up strings, instead of spreading out over the ground. This saves space and makes it easier to scout and identify pests that attack these crops. This method also keeps more of the leaves in the sunlight, which in turn means better growth.

In the desert area, scientists are also learning how to grow various edible plants called halophytes. These plants are adapted to growing in salty soils. A new source of food might be created if these plants could be grown along the world's thirty thousand miles of desert coastline. Ordinary seawater could then be used to irrigate them.

As the "Listen to the Land" boat passes into the third greenhouse area, the Creative Greenhouse, visitors see some of the imaginative techniques scientists are experimenting with in an attempt to grow food in more advantageous ways. The primary theme is that to meet our future food needs, we must not be limited to old ideas and ways of doing things but should continuously seek creative and imaginative new approaches.

One technique displayed here is to grow plants without using any soil at all. The plants may be grown hydroponically, in stationary water baths that are rich in nutrients. Or they may be grown on conveyor belts with their roots hanging in the air. Carried on the belts, the traveling plants get the proper amount of sunlight and are rotated through a root spray containing water and nutrients. Water hyacinths growing below the plants catch waste nutrients dripping down from the plants' roots and are then processed to produce methane gas. This, in turn, can be used to fuel the conveyor system. Systems like this, in which one plant feeds or helps another in some way, not only save existing resources, but create new ones.

Future farmers will not only be working here on earth, they will also undoubtedly be farming in colonies in outer space. Scientists have already

In the Desert Greenhouse at The Land, young tomato plants grow in sand (above). They will climb up the strings, making maximum use of vertical space.

Below, in another view of the Desert Greenhouse, *Euphorbia latyris,* a possible source of gasoline in the future, can be seen growing beyond the cactus.

In The Land cucumbers grow on space-saving
A-frames above lettuce. The lettuce is supported
by boards that float on a nutrient solution.

begun to experiment with ways of growing crops in space.

One such experiment is on display in the Creative Greenhouse. Lettuce plants are grown in great drums that revolve around central sources of light. The drums spin twenty-four hours a day, seven days a week, to provide a substitute force for the earth's gravity, which would of course not be present in space.

Because costs are high, greenhouse gardening must make the maximum use of available space. Many of the plants grown here have been specially bred for compactness. Others have been specially designed to grow vertically instead of horizontally. Scientists at The Land change the greenhouses periodically to experiment with new plants and new ways to grow them.

Learning about Nutrition

After taking the boat ride and observing The Land's creative and ingenious growing techniques, visitors can enjoy the lighthearted but serious look at nutrition provided by the Kitchen Kabaret exhibit. Just as important as increasing the world's food production is the task of making sure that people get the most nutritional benefit from the foods they eat. The Kitchen Kabaret revue provides an entertaining course in the basics of healthy eating. Against the background of a huge kitchen, dazzling *Audio-Animatronics*™ characters expound on the four main food groups that should be represented in the daily diet: the milk and cheese group; the cereal and bread group; the meat, poultry, fish, and beans group; and the fruit and vegetable group. Together these foods contain all the nutrients needed to build, repair, and maintain the human body.

Scientific knowledge of what makes up a balanced diet is fairly new. Through most of history good nutrition was more a matter of circumstance than anything else. Those people whose native agriculture was varied were able to eat enough of the right foods. This meant they were more likely to survive and pass on their eating habits to the next generation. Those whose diets were seriously lacking in one way or another usually died young or suffered severe illnesses.

Looking toward the day when food will be produced in space, workers at The Land grow lettuce in a drum (top) that spins to provide a substitute force to earth's gravity. The column pots, above, contain young pepper plants that will later be moved to the rotating conveyors in the background; rotation assures uniform light.

It was not until the mid-nineteenth century that the science of nutrition was born. Its originator was Baron Justus von Liebig, a German chemist who studied and classified nutrients. Von Liebig found that there were three classes of nutrients people needed in large amounts—carbohydrates, fats, and proteins. And there was one class of micronutrients needed in small amounts—vitamins and minerals.

Audio-Animatronics™ figures explain the benefits of a balanced diet in The Land's Kitchen Kabaret revue.

Carbohydrates include sugar, starches, and fibers. They are literally the staff of life because they provide the body with its main source of energy. They are the fuel that runs the body's engine. Carbohydrates make up some 65 percent of the average diet around the world. Almost all carbohydrates come from plant foods, such as cereal grains, sugarcane, potatoes, peas, apples, bananas, and all the other fruits and vegetables.

Fats perform a variety of critical tasks. They act as padding, or insulation, to prevent the body from losing too much heat. They cushion vital organs. They store energy. And they produce linoleic acid, which is essential to normal growth and healthy skin. Fats are found in abundance in animal foods such as meat, fish, dairy products, and eggs. They are also found in some plant foods, including nuts, olives, peanuts, and sunflower and flax seeds.

Proteins are the chief building blocks for skin, muscles, ligaments, blood, internal organs, hair, and nails. They are also essential to the formation of a variety of important body regulators, such as hormones and antibodies. Ideally, about 10 percent of all calories should come from proteins. Fish, meat, and dairy products are the main sources of protein for humans. Certain vegetables also offer a high protein content. But meat and vegetable proteins are not interchangeable. Meat provides all the chemicals needed to satisfy the body's protein requirements. No common vegetable—except the soybean—can do this by itself.

Ancient peoples had no way of knowing the shortcomings of vegetable proteins. Yet many basic native dishes combine vegetables so as to provide the complete protein requirement. The native American dish of corn and beans is one example. Peas and rice in Italy, and rice and lentils in India are others.

The final element in a complete and healthy nutrition program is the micronutrients—vitamins and minerals. There are thirteen different kinds of vitamins, chemical substances that are found in various foods. Vitamin C, for instance, is found in oranges and some other fruits and vegetables. Vitamins help the body to metabolize, or make proper use of, all the other nutrients. A lack of certain vitamins can lead to diseases such as scurvy, pellagra, rickets, and beriberi.

With so much now known about the science of nutrition, people can eat well even on a low budget. Guides to healthy eating are available from organizations such as the USDA's Human Nutrition Information Service and the Kraft Nutrition Advisory Council, which was the consultant on the Kitchen Kabaret. These organizations also study the nutritional value of new foods as they become available.

As the science of agriculture expands and develops and as agricultural production becomes more efficient, the goal of insuring that all of the world's people will enjoy a healthy diet becomes more and more realistic.

Merle H. Jensen, coordinator of programs at The Land and Arizona's Environmental Research Laboratory, has said of this task: "We can grow the world's required food if all nations and people work together, sharing new ideas. . . . It is our goal that The Land pavilion set the stage for this cooperation."

A Personal Involvement with Farming

The third exhibit at The Land, the inspiring motion picture *Symbiosis,* is shown at The Land's Harvest Theater. Like "Listen to the Land" and the Kitchen Kabaret, the purpose of this motion picture is to give the millions of visitors to The Land some sense of personal involvement in the world of farming and food production.

Henry A. Robitaille, director of the experimental growing areas at The Land, describes this aim: "Less than 5 percent of people in the United States are directly concerned with farming today. If you ask a first grader where his food comes from, he's likely to say the supermarket! We think

The creative partnership between man and the land, the subject of the motion picture *Symbiosis,* is exemplified by the lowland Dutch farms reclaimed from the sea (above) and by the Lapps, below, who nurture their reindeer and depend on them for life's necessities.

that's a great loss and we want to make it possible for anyone with curiosity to see the exciting things going on out there where food is really produced."

Symbiosis shows how humans throughout the world have had to respond to the specific environment they live in and in which all growth takes place. Viewers see some of the ingenious ways people have met the challenge of their surroundings.

In the Arctic, for instance, a family of Lapps herd reindeer across the snow-covered tundra. They carry on a way of life that has kept their people well fed and warmly clothed for more than two thousand years. In the highlands of Luzon, in the Philippines, Ifugao farmers tend terraced rice paddies that were carved out of steep mountainsides over three thousand years ago. In the Netherlands, Dutch farmers raise vegetables on polders, or lowland areas, that were reclaimed from the sea nine hundred years ago. And on an Egyptian oasis, *fellahs* (agricultural workers) water fields of millet and beans with a screw pump, following practices developed in ancient times.

Agriculture and the Environment

Each of these responses to the environment represents "the creative partnership" that René Dubos conceived of as a desirable goal for mankind. This partnership has allowed humans generation after generation to pursue a way of life that sustained them without upsetting the balance of their natural environment. In ancient times, humans were less likely to do damage to nature. This was so largely for two reasons. First, there were relatively few people competing for land and resources. Second, the technology used was simple and not really capable of changing the natural world to any great extent. As *Symbiosis* shows, however, developing civilizations brought changes that often served to harm the environment.

The Industrial Revolution that began in the second half of the eighteenth century led to an agricultural revolution, giving the farmer mechanized equipment that made it possible to "tame the wilderness." This term suggested that the land had become an adversary to be defeated instead of a partner in agricultural progress. Still, mechanized

equipment made it possible to cultivate millions of acres that had been tilled only lightly or had never felt the plow. Soil was treated as a resource that would last forever and remain unchanged. In fact, soil *is* relatively stable. Wherever the land is left in its natural state, soil is built up at more or less the same rate as it is used up. But farming tips the balance toward a more rapid loss of fertile soil. The greater the farming technology involved, the faster the soil loses its essential nutrients. Unless extra nutrients are added in the form of fertilizer, the soil gradually loses its usefulness. Cultivation also means there is a risk the soil will be rapidly eroded, or worn away. The farmer removes the earth's natural vegetation and loosens the soil in order to plant seeds. The soil is then left open to the eroding effects of wind and water. In addition, heavy farm machinery may thicken the soil into a heavy mass. This reduces its ability to hold air and water and makes it too solid to allow the growth of delicate roots. *(See Glossary, Erosion.)*

Mechanized farming brought great rises in productivity. But it also threatened nature's delicate balance, the relationship of water supply, fertile soil, and the growth of natural vegetation that supports continued agricultural success. Droughts, floods, erosion, and the invasions of pests were once occasional local disasters. Gradually they became serious world problems.

Today, we are witnessing a second agricultural revolution. Its aim is to restore the old partnership between people and the earth and to make this partnership work through the use of new methods of scientific farming. *Symbiosis* demonstrates this approach by showing how farmlands once lost through carelessness and ignorance are now being successfully reclaimed.

The narrator of *Symbiosis* delivers the motion picture's message in eloquent and poetic terms that every visitor to The Land should take to heart. His words reinforce a major theme of this exhibit: "Nothing in the universe exists alone. . . . Every drop of water, every human being, all creatures in the web of life, and all ideas in the web of knowledge are part of an immense, evolving, dynamic whole as old—and as young—as the universe itself."

Fish in Our Future

Fish represent only a tiny fraction of human food consumption today, largely because they are difficult and expensive to catch by traditional methods. But as visitors to The Land at EPCOT Center learn as they ride through the experimental Aquacell facility, controlled farming of fish and other aquatic plants and animals, called aquaculture, is expected to make an important contribution to the world's diet in the future.

Practiced as long ago as 2100 B.C. by the Chinese, who introduced carp into flooded rice fields, fish farming has only recently been the subject of concentrated scientific research. The many advantages of aquaculture are readily apparent. There are literally millions of acres of underused ponds, lakes, and irrigation ditches that might be turned into fish farms at minimum expense. In cool regions, there are bodies of water that are currently warmed by waste heat from power plants. Experiments have shown that these lagoons can be made productive if stocked with tropical fish such as the African tilapia, above left, a tasty fish that multiplies rapidly in both salt and freshwater.

Farm-raised fish can be far more profitable for the grower than livestock. They require little space, and since different species feed at different depths, it is often possible to raise two or three kinds in one pond.

Most commercial aquaculture today is conducted in warm areas outdoors, with catfish being the prime species raised in the United States. Typical yields per acre of pond average about three to five thousand pounds annually. Even more productive is raceway aquaculture. Raceways contain a uniform colony of fish or crustacea. Water is brought in at one end and either discarded or cleaned and recirculated at the other, so temperature, food, and waste removal can be precisely monitored. In an Environmental Research Laboratory project in Mexico, advanced aquaculture techniques have increased shrimp yields from two to fifty tons per acre.

Refinements of raceway culture are being studied. One technique is the use of red filters to modify sunlight reaching the fish, which is thought to reduce stress and result in faster growth. This technique is seen in the photograph at right of The Land aquacell.

Most aquaculture to date has focused on freshwater species, but scientists expect a boom in saltwater fish farming in the near future. Japan already raises shrimp, oysters, and seaweed commercially. And China, the world leader in aquaculture, already derives 40 percent of all its fish protein from farmed production.

CHAPTER 3

The Origins of Agriculture

Tracing how and why agriculture began—and pinpointing the time and place—is one of the most interesting problems that historians face. For thousands of years, early peoples found their food in nature. They hunted and fished and ate plants and fruits that grew wild. What led these people to invent farming, a completely different way of life? Did the idea come slowly? Or did it come all at once in a flash of inspiration? Did it originate with one tribe and then spread by example? Or was it invented over and over again in many different and isolated parts of the world where the people had no chance to copy other tribes? Which crops were planted first? Did they look and taste like the foods we eat today, or were they so different we wouldn't recognize them on a modern dining table?

Historians now believe that the process of gathering food in the wild, repeated over many thousands of years, created the conditions that led naturally to farming. They also believe that the development of farming was a very gradual process that occurred over several thousand years.

It happened over and over again in many different parts of the ancient world in response to similar conditions. In most cases, wild cereal grasses were the key to this dramatic change, though, in a few places, root crops and other vegetables may have been grown first. These wild plants then changed greatly as they became domesticated— planted and grown by people.

An American archaeologist, Richard S. Mac-Neish, has made a careful study of how and why tribes that once moved about to hunt and gather food became farmers who planted and tended crops in one place. MacNeish dug down through

An ancient wall painting shows the bounty of a well-tended Egyptian farm, around 1300 B.C. Barley, flax, and date palms are among the summer crops.

a series of campsites buried for centuries in Mexico's Tehuacán valley. These campsites date back some seven thousand years ago, to around 5000 B.C. His investigations led him to propose an explanation for the rise of farming that has been widely accepted.

The Life of Paleolithic Man

To understand how and why farming began, we must first look at the life of paleolithic man. The paleolithic period is the earliest and longest period of human development. It began about two million years ago and lasted until about ten thousand years ago. The first peoples that can reasonably be called human appeared at that time. These first humans lived much as the other animals did. They hunted wild beasts for food and they ate wild plants. It was a simple existence whose success or failure was measured by the survival of the individual and the small tribal group.

These early people owned only a few stone tools and the rude clothing on their backs. They had great respect for the natural world around them. But they did not settle down on one plot of land. Instead, they moved from place to place.

The change from wandering hunter-gatherer into farmer presented new possibilities and new problems. The first farmers probably continued to get a large part of their diet from wild things. But because they could grow food, these early peoples now had a personal or communal stake in a piece of land, at least for part of the year.

Eventually this change created a whole new way of life for human beings. Unlike the nomad, or wanderer, the farmer had the urge to improve his immediate surroundings. He began to build more permanent structures and to accumulate varied possessions. With his food supply made more secure, he was much more inclined to plan for the future. As agriculture flourished, and the community grew, its members began to develop more specialized skills. Women often became the day-

A ceramic urn, created by Zapotec craftsman of Mexico around A.D. 500, celebrates the corn god Pitao Cozobi. The Zapotecs were highland farmers.

to-day tenders of the fields, while men herded and cared for the community's semidomesticated animals. With a new sense of his self and his worth, the earliest farmer began to create rituals and traditions relating to the seasonal cultivation of food crops. These made him feel more secure and powerful. From these and other changes different kinds of civilizations eventually grew.

How Farming Began

In his research, MacNeish was able to learn many of the specifics of how this process occurred. His work indicates that the wandering hunter-gatherers returned each year to areas where they knew they would find a good food supply. In the case of the Tehuacán valley in Mexico, the food source was a kind of squash that grows in abundance. The meat of this squash happens to be bitter. But the seeds, which are carried in separate pod cases, are tasty and nourishing, and the hunter-gatherers liked to pick them.

This was not quite as easy as it sounds. At the moment the seeds became ripe the pods exploded—popping out seeds in all directions. This is nature's way of spreading the seeds of wild plants so that new plants can take root and grow. But for man it makes harvesting seeds difficult. Most of the seeds the hunter-gatherers managed to harvest belonged to plants with seedpods that did not explode quite so readily. In nature a difference such as this in a plant or animal is known as a genetic mutation, an alteration in the genes of the organism. The squash plant with good seed-popping ability did the best job of reproducing more plants like itself, since its seeds were scattered over a wider area. A plant whose seeds popped less easily, on the other hand, would reproduce less of its kind. Eventually such a plant might even die out altogether.

Three illustrations from a Peruvian manuscript depict tasks in an Inca community. At left, a farmer prepares holes with a digging stick as women set seed; center, a worker tends the irrigation system; right, the harvest is taken to the granary.

The hunter-gatherers brought the squash seeds back to their camp. Here, without quite knowing what they were doing, they took the first steps toward becoming farmers. As they ate the seeds, they scattered some on the ground. Others were discarded on the camp garbage dump. Some of the scattered seeds germinated, or began to grow, producing new squash plants. In this way, the hunter-gatherers began to cultivate a new breed of semiwild squash plants.

With a wild garden of squash plants growing at their seasonal campsite, the hunter-gatherers began to take much more of an interest in the site and in the well-being of their food source. They had always believed that their survival was due to the powers of spirits. Now they gave thanks to the deities of fertility and the harvest.

At the same time, members of the band tried to protect their new food source in practical ways. They cut back and weeded out the less healthy-looking plants. They found that this simple experiment caused the other plants to grow bigger and stronger. They noted that drooping plants suddenly flourished after a rainfall. So they tried watering the plants themselves during dry spells. When they saw that especially healthy plants grew in the camp garbage dump, they may have begun to throw their own waste materials on the garden plants and fertilized them in this way.

Eventually they realized that seeds planted in earth that had been turned over had a better chance of growing. So they began to scratch the earth with a digging stick and plant seeds deliberately. Success with one kind of plant like squash led them to experiment with other kinds. In time, something very much like a garden plot must have been marked off in the camp and perhaps even protected by a fence.

All of the care devoted to the camp garden plots resulted in the growth of highly productive squash plants. But it also tended to make the plants less able to survive in a totally wild environment. For instance, fewer and fewer of the plants grown by the hunter-gatherers had exploding seedpods.

Over many years and many generations of plants, the end result was a new kind of squash plant. It was no longer a wild squash plant, but one that was domesticated. Without the help of humans, it could not grow to maturity or scatter its seeds to reproduce. The hunter-gatherer had become a farmer in the full sense of the word.

All of this did not happen overnight, of course. MacNeish's explanation represents a simplified version of a process that probably took thousands of years. Even so, it is very likely that the change from a hunter-gatherer society to an agricultural society followed a pattern similar to this in many different areas of the world.

The Earliest Farmers

Where did farming first begin? The evidence suggests that it did not start in the fertile river valleys, such as the Nile River valley, where wild foods were abundant. Instead, farming probably began in hilly, semidesert areas, where finding food was a problem. Here, animals sought by hunters were in short supply. This may have been because of the extinction of some species. Or it may have been because of competition between bands of hunters. Food shortages naturally led to changes in diet. The people were forced to eat plants they had not previously tried or had rejected.

Among the earliest farmers were people living in the Middle East. Here, in the foothills that curve northward from Israel and Jordan to Syria, Turkey, Iraq, and Iran, evidence has been found of a number of small farming villages dating from between 7000 and 8000 B.C. Archaeologists have dug up several of these villages and found that domesti-

cated varieties of emmer wheat and barley had become part of the basic food supply. There was also evidence that domesticated goats and sheep had become part of the food supply.

By roughly 5000 B.C., farming and the herding of animals had become established in other areas, including Southeast Asia, Mesopotamia, the Levant, Anatolia, mainland Greece, and possibly some of the larger islands of the eastern Mediterranean. At the same time, Indians in the highlands of Mexico were growing squash, beans, and avocados and also raising an early version of domesticated corn. And natives of the Andes Mountains in Peru were growing potatoes.

A thousand years later, cereals were being farmed in such far-flung areas as northern China, the Indus Valley, the North African coast, Egypt's Nile Valley, and along the banks of the Danube River and up into central Europe. By 3000 B.C., primitive farming was being practiced throughout most of continental Europe and the British Isles.

Along with the establishment of a farming economy came new tools and new ways of farming. Most early farming was done in light upland soils. In these soils, the sharp, pointed digging sticks used by the farmer's hunter-gatherer ancestors to dig up root vegetables were still valuable tools. The earliest farmers used them to stir up the earth and prepare holes for planting. Later, the farmers made stone spades, hoes, sickles, and scythes to speed the work and increase human muscle power.

The upland soils were easy to work, but they also tended to erode, or wear away, their fertility rather quickly. A certain crop would grow vigorously for a couple of years. Then, mysteriously, the size of the crop would be reduced in the third year. And in the fourth year, the plants would grow even smaller in size.

Today, we know the reason for this. Nutrients, nourishing elements that keep the soil healthy, were being taken away faster than they were being put back. Early farmers did not understand this scientifically, of course. But still they began to practice a primitive form of crop rotation. They did this by abandoning fields when they became unproductive and growing their crops on other sites.

A generation later, their children might return to plant the unused fields once more. Having lain fallow, or unplanted, for some time, the fields had regained their fertility. In some communities the unused fields were given over to flocks of livestock as pastureland. This increased their fertility, as the animals' waste droppings helped to enrich the soil.

To enrich the soil in other areas, such as the tropical jungles of Central America and Peru, farmers used a method known as "slash and burn," still practiced today. They cleared small

Chinese rice cultivation in the eighteenth century was still much as it had been for a thousand years. At left, a peasant transplants seedlings in a flooded paddy. Below, two workers reap the harvest while others gather the crop into sheaves. Threshing, husking, and winnowing follow.

patches of forest by halting the growth of large trees and cutting down smaller ones. Then they burned the trees. This left wood ashes on top of the earth, which added nutrients such as potassium to soil that otherwise was of poor quality for agriculture.

The first farmers also practiced plant improvement. Though they did not really understand the art, the farmers simply used their common sense. When they wanted to breed new plants they gen-erally selected the seeds or roots of the fattest, largest, tastiest plants and discarded the weaker, less hardy plants. In time, most of the weaker ancestors of various types of plants died out altogether.

Wild corn, the ancestor of today's hybrid corn, is a classic example of a less productive variety that died out. Communities also exchanged plants, and this increased the variety of foods available in virtually every part of the world.

One man steers the plow and another goads the animals as the light soil of an Egyptian farm is turned over at the start of the growing season.

The Development of Irrigation

Still greater strides were made when farming became a way of life among the people living along the banks of the great Tigris, Euphrates, and Nile rivers. There, the climate was hot and dry. But the rivers provided water, the one vital element the climate lacked. Communities in these river valleys invented a number of ingenious irrigation and drainage systems to serve the needs of their farmers.

There were no earlier waterworks for the river valley farmers to copy or develop. They had to start from scratch. No doubt earlier upland farmers had scraped out shallow channels in the hillsides to coax rivulets of precious mountain springs and streams toward their fields. But along the banks of the rivers, known as the food plains, the problems were much more difficult. To begin with, the rivers were large and periodically overflowed their banks and flooded the fields. In one way this was of vital help to the farmers. Along with the water, the rivers dropped a nutrient-rich layer of mud, or topsoil, on the fields. This meant that the farmers could grow fine, healthy crops and not have to abandon their fields after a few years because the soil had become lifeless. But the floods also threatened to wash crops away and destroy villages.

A system to control the flooding needed to be developed. In addition, fields needing irrigation were more often above the river level than below it. To use the river water, some means of carrying water uphill was needed.

The ancient Sumerians, who lived on the plains of Mesopotamia around 4000 B.C., were probably the first people to invent ways of controlling and delivering water for crop growth. The neighboring Egyptians soon followed their example. Ancient writings refer to the building of canals, dams, reservoirs, and dikes. The Sumerians and Egyptians used these devices for controlling, storing, and directing the flow of water for their fields.

To ease the labor of irrigating fields, the Egyptian farmer at left used a *shaduf*, a device that lifts water from the river by means of a bucket and counterweight.

Early Egyptian writings also refer to a device for lifting water, the *shaduf*. It consisted of a post with a long counterweighted beam attached to it in the form of a T. At the end of the beam was a bucket. The farmer or one of his helpers lowered one end of the beam so that the bucket dipped into the river. The farmer then lowered the counterweighted end of the beam, lifting the bucket as high as six feet, then swung the beam around to an irrigation ditch to empty the water. A farmer could raise as much as six hundred gallons of water a day using a *shaduf*.

Whenever such irrigation methods were invented and used, they fostered the development of the communities. The use of advanced hydraulics, or water engineering, could only exist in a society that had a strong central government. Such water projects had to be planned, built, and directed. They were too complicated to be organized by farmers alone. They needed engineers capable of inventing such systems. And they needed recognized laws to govern how the supply of water would be shared among the farmers. There had to be clerks to keep records and a calendar advanced enough to keep track of seasonal rainfalls and temperatures. Large teams of farmers and other workers had to be organized to do the actual building and to maintain the canals. In short, irrigation and drainage could only be undertaken in an organized society.

The widespread use of irrigation naturally increased the amount of land that could be cultivated and the productivity that could be achieved on that land. It also meant that a lot of human labor was needed. The more days spent working on the dikes, the fewer days the farmers had available to work in the fields.

New and Better Tools

To fill the gap, inventors had to come up with more efficient tools. One such tool was the hand plow, which was probably developed as early as

The apple harvest is celebrated in this fifth-century B.C. Greek vase. The modern apple probably originated as a wild fruit in the Caucasus region (now part of the Soviet Union) and was introduced to Greece and the rest of the world by migrants. The Greeks, however, gave credit for the apple to their goddess of agriculture, Demeter.

5000 B.C. The hand plow was no more than a forked wooden stick or kind of rough hoe made of the hardest wood available. The farmer dragged this simple tool behind him, cutting a shallow but continuous furrow through the topsoil. The two chief goals of plowing were to pulverize the soil and to conserve moisture. In the arid regions where these tools first appeared, the farmer typically plowed his field twice. The second time he plowed at right angles to the first. In this way a farmer prepared the land for seeding without exposing the moister earth beneath the surface.

Then, sometime after 4000 B.C., someone realized that animals such as oxen could be used to increase the plowman's efficiency. The traction plow then came into being. The earliest ox-drawn plows consisted of a forked branch only slightly larger than the hand plow. Its "plowing end" was shaped like a primitive plowshare. The farmer held the two long forks of the traction plow as the animals pulled forward on a rope tied to their horns. The farmer steered the plow and pressed it downward so it sliced the earth into straight, even rows. In time the oxen's harness became a wooden yoke and the rope became a pole. The plow itself gradually became heavier, stronger, and more advanced. An iron share blade and a gadget that dropped seeds into the furrow were among the many improvements made on it. The old system of crossplowing remained, though. It was still the best way to prepare the light dry soils.

After the invention of the traction plow, farming changed very little in the ancient world for the next two thousand years. There were just two notable developments. First, farmers planted more new crops. Second, they found a new way to keep soil fertile. Known as the two-field rotation system, it was developed by the Romans, who then carried it to every corner of their large empire. Under this system, farmers cultivated only half of their land each year, leaving the other half to lie fallow.

As the Roman Empire declined in the fifth century, northern Europe began to experience its own agricultural revolution. New methods were needed because the ancient ways did not suit the environmental conditions there. For one thing, northern soils were heavy and sticky. It took rainwater a longer time to filter down through these soils. The traction plow was introduced to the north through Roman conquest and trade. But it was not strong enough to cut the heavy earth, nor to peel it back in order to let it dry and break up. Farmers had to labor hard and long, and the crops they produced were poor compared to those in southern areas.

A breakthrough came sometime around A.D. 600, probably in eastern Europe. Here a farmer invented a clever new machine, a heavy plow that ran on wheels. It had a colter, or knife, to open up a furrow. It had a share to slice under the earth. And it had a moldboard to turn the loosened ribbon of earth aside. This compound plow prepared the earth more effectively in one pass than a scratch plow did in two passes. Over the next few centuries, it was introduced into western Europe, where it made possible the cultivation of vast areas of previously untouched soil. This, in turn, meant that very primitive communities could learn a new way of life and grow their own food.

A Changing Way of Life

During the Middle Ages, the compound plow played a major role in shaping the way of life in Europe. The heavy plow required eight oxen to pull it, compared to two for the traction plow. An individual peasant could not afford the expense of running this new plow. Instead, groups of peasants pooled their oxen and their labor. This meant that some system of organization had to be set up, and village councils developed to oversee the communal effort.

Besides being heavy and expensive to run, the new plows were also very cumbersome. They could not operate well in small spaces or turn easily at the end of each row. Up to this time, plots of land had traditionally been small squarish fields, with each farmer tending his own land. Now the private plots gave way to larger strip fields owned by the community. The fields were separated from each other simply by unplowed ridges.

The use of the heavy compound plow led to a rise in the amount of crops grown per acre. This led farmers seeking even larger crops gradually to abandon the two-field system that had been used since Roman times as a way of resting the land.

There was another reason for abandoning the two-field system. Farmers in northern Europe realized that their land did not need to lie fallow as often as every second year; they plowed it so deeply that nutrient-rich soil was continually turned up. A new system, called three-field rotation, became the rule. The farmers planted one field with wheat or rye in the fall and harvested it in the spring. They planted another field in the spring with peas or barley and harvested it in the fall. They left a third field to lie fallow for a season to recover its fertility. Then, in rotation, it would become the field planted in the fall and the field planted in the spring. With more fields in use, farmers could grow a greater variety of crops. This, in turn, led to increased variety in the medieval diet.

Farming was affected by other changes as well. One was the use of the improved, padded horse collar and horseshoe, both of which were imported from central Asia sometime before A.D. 1000. Before that time, farmers found horses to be unsatisfactory as draft animals, that is, animals used to pull a load. Actually, the problem was the earlier harness, or yoke, not the horse. Though the yoke fit oxen well enough, it was completely wrong for the horse's anatomy. Much of the burden of pulling was placed on the horse's chest and windpipe. This meant the animal could exert no more than one-fourth its strength. The new harness fit properly and quickly made the more energetic, more maneuverable horse the draft animal of choice. New horseshoes made of iron also helped. They improved the horse's grip on the earth while protecting its fragile hooves.

In the medieval Book of Hours at left traditional farming activities for March are depicted. Hoeing, digging, and plowing begin the planting season.

Conceived in the East and improved in the West, the medieval horse collar enabled the horse to pull greater loads by distributing the weight more evenly.

Another invention that changed farming was the windmill, which was first used in Europe in the twelfth century. It had many uses as a source of power. But for the farmer, its most important use was in large drainage projects. By pumping off water from once unusable swamps and marshes, the windmill turned vast areas into fertile fields.

The Limits of Productivity

The productivity of farming increased gradually throughout the Middle Ages. A number of advances led to this result, including more effective plows, better draft animals, and more efficient use of manpower. The opening up of woods and wetlands to farming also led to increased crop production.

But finally, in about the twelfth century, productivity began to level off. It would advance very little for some seven hundred years, until scientific knowledge increased and industrial farming methods were introduced.

The average peasant of the twelfth century could probably produce about 200 percent more food than his ancestors. Even so, the average yield from sowing two bushels of wheat over a one-acre field was only ten bushels. (Wheat fields in the United States today yield an average of forty bushels per acre.)

Europe's farmers were more advanced than farmers in other parts of the world. But, as late as the eighteenth century, they were still just beginning to develop the agricultural potential of the land. The real excitement lay ahead, in a time when a new agricultural revolution would shake the earth.

GIFT FOR THE GRANGERS

"I PAY FOR ALL."

FAITH, HOPE, CHARITY, FIDELITY

CHAPTER 4

The Nineteenth-Century Revolution

From the birth of agriculture some ten thousand years ago up to the early nineteenth century, the farmer's ability to produce food advanced very little. Productivity ultimately depended chiefly on human muscle power and the number of hours in the working day. Draft animals eased the job of plowing, but they ate so much feed that there was only a slight advantage in using them on most farms. In any event, the farmer still had to put in long hours doing such chores as weeding, harrowing, reaping, threshing, and gathering the crops—all requiring tedious hand labor. In general, the farmer's life was what it had always been —a life of unending work and hardship. After all his efforts, the farmer raised only enough to feed his family and a handful of other people living nearby. Still, farming was the dominant way of life for most of the world's people and it seemed likely to remain so.

Then came the beginnings of scientific agriculture, and almost everything about farming began to change. One of the earliest experimenters was Jethro Tull, an English gentleman farmer (someone who farms for pleasure rather than profit). Around 1701, Tull designed and built a horse-drawn hoe for weeding. He also developed a mechanical seed drill. Normally, farmers simply scattered seeds when they sowed their fields. But by using a machine that drilled holes in the earth and then deposited a seed at the proper depth, the farmer cut down on wastage.

In later years, Tull wrote several influential books on the principles of cultivating land and growing crops. He described the importance of preparing and conditioning the soil, of planting seeds by drilling, and of planting in rows. Tull's experiments were aimed mainly at improving scientific practices in raising crops. If these practices were fol-

The Grange movement grew in response to hard times among American farmers in the 1860s and 70s. The farmers joined together to oppose the railroad and grain elevator monopolies.

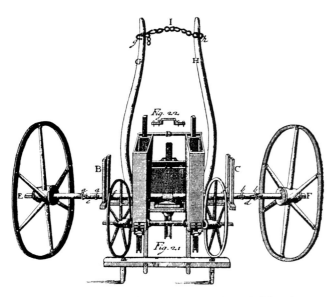

Jethro Tull, a British inventor, introduced this wheat drill, the first of its kind, in 1701. It opened furrows, sowed, and covered the seed in one operation.

lowed, he maintained, farmers were sure to achieve increased harvests for each unit of land they farmed.

Other experimenters saw that farming could be made much more productive through the use of labor-saving devices and cheap power. They eventually produced what are now considered to be the classic inventions of the modern era of agriculture —the plow, the reaper, and the tractor.

The first real breakthrough in the design of farm implements occurred in the United States in 1797, when Charles Newbold of New Jersey patented a one-piece cast-iron plowshare. Many people thought that iron poisoned the soil, so Newbold's device was not greeted with enthusiasm. But a few people realized that cast-iron plowshares were much better than wood-and-iron ones. Thomas Jefferson, the future president, was one of them. Using careful mathematical calculations, Jefferson designed a new iron moldboard, the curved plate of the plow that turns over the earth as the plow digs a furrow. Jefferson carefully designed the curvature so that the plow dug deeper with less effort. Jefferson's new design, as well as his scientific approach, were acclaimed and studied by learned societies in America and in Europe.

In 1819, Jethro Wood of New York patented a sectional cast-iron plow with a moldboard design that was even more efficient than Jefferson's. His plow had an additional feature: as its parts wore out, they could be replaced.

These first American plows worked quite well in turning over rocky eastern soils. But they still required a lot of labor. It took four oxen and three men to operate Wood's plow smoothly. One man had to drive the team of oxen, another had to steer the plow, and a third had to knock off clumps of soil as they got caught on the blade. Used on the prairies of the Midwest, Wood's plow was far less successful. The prairie's six-foot-high grass, four-inch-deep sod, and heavy soil made plowing extremely difficult.

An Illinois blacksmith, John Deere, came to the prairie farmer's rescue. Deere had been experimenting with a variety of plow designs. One day in 1837, he happened to find a discarded mill saw blade made of the hardest Sheffield steel. Deere worked it into the shape of a moldboard. It sheared right through the heavy, sticky sod. Deere promptly introduced the "self-polishing" steel moldboard. Soon it was being used on all kinds of plows and for all kinds of soil conditions.

The Age of Mechanization

A few years earlier, in 1831, Cyrus H. Mc-Cormick had produced the mechanical reaper. This horse-drawn machine combined the jobs of cutting and gathering ripe grain in one quick and easy operation. Traditionally, a farmer had to cut the grain by hand with a scythe. As it was cut, the grain fell into a device consisting of wooden ribs, like the tines of a fork, that was attached to the scythe. This device was called a cradle. A farmer using a cradle might cut and gather two acres of grain per day. The McCormick reaper could cut as many as twelve, fifteen, or even twenty acres under the best conditions.

As the nineteenth century progressed, other inventors devised machines that mechanized such laborious jobs as manure spreading, seeding, cultivating, hulling, binding, mowing, husking, and threshing. The new machines increased the size and value of the harvest, and on this basis, they were not really expensive. In 1846, a small horse-drawn cultivator cost from $5 to $8. In 1857, a "self-raking reaper-mower" cost $200. In 1853, a horse-powered thresher, invented by J. I. Case, sold for $280. Advertisements claimed the ma-

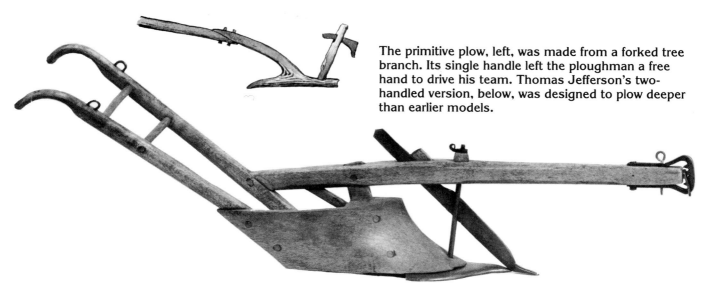

The primitive plow, left, was made from a forked tree branch. Its single handle left the ploughman a free hand to drive his team. Thomas Jefferson's two-handled version, below, was designed to plow deeper than earlier models.

In the 1860s, Deere & Co. of Moline, Illinois, offered the horse-drawn "iron beam" plow, above, featuring a sturdy iron beam and a steel plowshare tailored to the midwestern prairie. A few decades later, tractor-drawn gang plows like the one below could open several furrows at once, reducing labor still further.

James Oliver of South Bend, Indiana, offered the first version of this plow in 1869. Its chilled steel moldboard was allegedly far less brittle than those made from cast steel, and because it was smoother, it could turn the earth more readily.

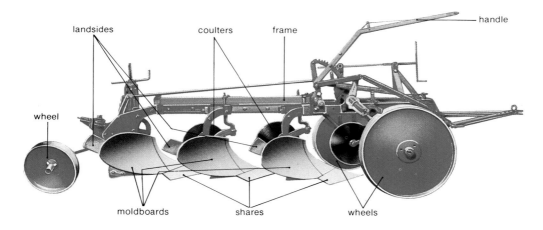

landsides   coulters   frame   handle

wheel

moldboards   shares   wheels

chine could thresh "from 250 to 400 bushels of wheat in a day, or twice the quantity of oats, and clean fit for market without waste." In contrast, using the older method of threshing grain by treading it on the barn floor, two men and six horses could produce about one hundred bushels in a day. A significant amount of the crop would be lost in the process.

As the frontier for farming moved farther west, the trend toward mechanization speeded up.

Farms became larger and more specialized, concentrating on one or two major crops. They also became commercial, growing food to sell rather than to feed the family.

As a result of increasing mechanization, some farmers in the Midwest joined forces at critical times in the growing season to share equipment. The group of farmers would run small armadas of machines across their fields. One extremely large farm, the Cass-Cheney Bonanza Farm in the Da-

kota Territory's Red River Valley, used thirty steam engines, fifty-three threshing machines, one hundred gang plows, eighty seeders, and two hundred reapers, plus eight hundred horses and mules. The animals and equipment worked thirty thousand acres and harvested some six hundred thousand bushels of spring wheat. Out in the far West, on the vast grain farms of Oregon and Washington, gigantic machines called Holt combines were put to use in the 1880s. A single com-

bine might need as many as thirty horses to pull it. But the machine earned its keep. It could cut a standing crop in a path from sixteen to twenty-four feet wide, then thresh, clean, and sack the grain in one operation.

The steam engines at the Bonanza Farm were increasingly used instead of draft animals. They were set up on stationary platforms or hauled about on huge wagons with an equally bulky fuel supply following behind them. They could be harnessed to run threshers, winnowers, power saws, and some dairying equipment. But they were still too cumbersome for most farms. Self-propelled gasoline-powered engines were another matter. No sooner did they become available than just about every farmer wanted one.

By 1892, the first successful tractor, built by John Froelich, was put to use in the wheat fields of South Dakota. This nine-thousand-pound machine had a simple two-cycle, one-cylinder internal combustion engine, which produced some thirty horsepower, more than twice that of the heavier steam engines then available. And it did so with its own self-contained fuel supply. In 1903 the first tractor-manufacturing company was formed in Charles City, Iowa. By 1914, there were about thirty manufacturers and they had sold some seventeen thousand engines to America's farmers. Just six years later, in 1920, the number had soared to 246,000. The machines did everything from plowing and harrowing to harvesting grain and pumping water. The gas-powered machines did more than just save labor. By replacing draft animals, they made it possible for farmers to grow food for humans on ninety million acres previously devoted to producing animal feed.

The Land-Rich American Farmer

The spirit of Yankee inventiveness certainly deserves some credit for the rush of technological advances that occurred in nineteenth-century America. But there were other reasons for the in-

A Pennsylvania harvest festival around 1853 begins with the boiling of apples. Some of the fruit will be made into a beverage, some into apple butter.

The Farmer's Chores

Farming is a more complicated process than many people think. Here are definitions of some of the operations farmers perform in order to produce their crops.

Plowing: *Cutting and partly pulverizing the soil to prepare it for planting.*

Harrowing: *Breaking up or evening up the soil after plowing.*

Planting, Seeding: *Putting seeds in the ground in a regular pattern, usually in rows, and covering the seeds with earth.*

Cultivating: *Breaking up the soil among growing crops to aerate it, conserve moisture, and control weeds.*

Weeding: *Controlling weeds by digging them out physically with a cultivator, harrow, hoe, or other tool, or by applying chemical herbicides that kill them.*

Hoeing: *Using a hoe to cultivate the soil around plants or to remove weeds.*

Fertilizing: *Applying fertilizer to crops or to the soil to promote crop growth.*

Irrigating: *Applying water to crops or to the soil to promote crop growth.*

Harvesting: *Gathering in a crop by picking it (tomatoes, fruits) or cutting it (grains, grasses).*

Reaping: *Harvesting grain or grasses by cutting them with a scythe or a reaping machine.*

Mowing: *Cutting grain or grasses to harvest them.*

Threshing: *Separating out the grain or seed from a crop such as wheat by stepping on it (treading), rubbing it, striking it with a flail, or using a threshing machine.*

Husking: *Removing the protective husk or other seed covering from a crop such as corn or rice.*

Winnowing: *Separating the grain from the chaff—the unwanted seed covering—by tossing it in the air and letting the wind carry the unwanted material away.*

novations, and they continue to shape farming today. Probably the major reason was the shortage of manpower. The traditional kinds of farming practiced in densely populated Europe and Asia required many workers. In America there were just too few hands to work the vast tracts of virgin land in this way.

Even if there had been enough workers, though, the typical nineteenth-century American farmer had little incentive to aim for high yields per acre using careful techniques. He could earn greater profits by farming "extensively," that is, by cultivating more land. Tracts of fertile land were dozens and sometimes hundreds of times larger in the United States than in Europe. American land was usually "dirt cheap"—indeed, some of the best property was free. The Homestead Act of 1862 gave settlers tracts of 160 acres (one-fourth of a square mile) as long as they stayed for five years and made certain minimal improvements. This meant that just about anyone who wanted to farm could have his own place. In a few years, 147 million acres of western lands were broken up into something like 1.6 million family farms. Often the farmer's only helpers were members of the family. Not surprisingly, then, the land-rich, labor-poor American homesteader welcomed every advance in mechanization.

Even "limitless" land must inevitably come to an end, and soil overused and misused must in time begin to lose its fertility. By the 1890s, there were few fertile corners of America that had not been laid claim to or that were not showing some signs of soil depletion. The conclusion was inescapable. Farmers had to seek higher yields per acre. It was at this point that agricultural science, engineering, and education came to the aid of the American farmer.

Producing Higher Yields

Chemists were among the first scientists to apply basic research to agriculture. They studied the relationship between plant growth and the fertility of the soil. The first revelation came in Germany in the 1830s when Baron Justus von Liebig found that plants get their nourishment from a combination of chemicals in the air and chemicals in the soil. The amount of nitrogen, phosphorus, and potassium in the soil is limited, so the farmer who wants to insure that his crops grow vigorously must add a new supply of these nutrients in the form of "artificial manures," or fertilizers. Von Liebig also found that each kind of plant makes unique demands upon the soil. This means that if the same kind of plant is grown year after year in the same earth, some nutrients will be depleted more than if crops of different sorts are rotated.

Farmer-mechanic Cyrus McCormick was twenty-two when he gave the first public demonstration of his revolutionary mechanical reaper.

THE TESTING OF THE FIRST REAPING MACHINE NEAR STEELE'S TAVERN. VA. A.D. 1831.

Olaf Kranz, a member of the Bishop Hill communal farm in Illinois, painted these scenes around 1875.
Plowing (above) and sowing (below) involved the whole community.

To assure straight corn rows, men stretch a knotted rope across the field as women mark the spaces with hoes. Below, men cut grain with scythes as women gather it.

Supplies of inexpensive manufactured fertilizers became available in 1842 when an Englishman, John Bennet Lawes, patented a process for producing phosphates by treating naturally occurring phosphate rock with sulphuric acid. Lawes's process made possible large-scale production, and manufacture began soon after in Europe and the United States. In the second half of the nineteenth century, commercial production of other kinds of fertilizers also began. Among these were nitrates, compounds containing nitrogen, and potash, a compound containing potassium. At the same time, many farmers developed a better understanding of the value of natural organic waste materials in maintaining the soil's fertility. They began to use wood ashes, ground-up bones (bonemeal), and lime for this purpose.

The first scientific work in breeding new varieties of plants also began in the mid-nineteenth century. Early efforts involved carefully selecting parent plants for size and color and health in order to improve the vigor and variety of offspring. Prog-

With thirty horses and only a half dozen men, a giant Holt combine reaps, threshes, cleans, and sacks as many as forty-five acres of wheat daily. The photograph below was taken in Oregon in the 1880s.

An early gas-powered tractor pulls a gang plow across the plains of eastern Oregon. Combustion engines succeeded steam engines beginning in the 1890s.

ress was slow because the scientific basis of inheritance was not widely known until well into the twentieth century. (See "Gregor Mendel: Man of Breeding," page 68.) But significant breakthroughs were made.

Probably the most famous American plant experimenter was Luther Burbank. A farm boy who had no scientific training, Burbank spent fifty years hybridizing, or crossbreeding, what he called "creations," new plants that he bred from varieties of existing ones. He launched his career when he developed a new variety of potato, the Burbank, in the early 1870s. He went on to create many new varieties of plums, prunes, apples, cherries, peaches, quinces, nectarines, tomatoes, sweet corn, squashes, asparagus, and other fruits and vegetables in his laboratories in Santa Rosa, California. (See "The Plant Wizard," page 58.)

A number of other Americans also worked steadily to improve the yield of such staple crops as corn and wheat and make them better able to resist diseases. Biologists roamed the world to bring back seeds of new food and fiber plants for use in America. Careful studies were also made on how to improve livestock. Scientists began by breeding meatier, healthier pigs. Progress was then made on developing improved breeds of cattle, sheep, and other animals.

Fighting Pests and Disease

Work also proceeded on ways to control pests. In the eighth century B.C., the Greek poet Homer noted that the Greeks used sulfur to rid their houses of pests. Since that time, farmers had used many common substances, such as nicotine, sulfur, soap, arsenic, and pyrethrum—the dried flowers of the Chrysanthemum family—to fight pests. Now scientists tried to discover how poisons such as arsenic actually worked, in order to make wider use of them. In 1867, for example, farmers began to use a new arsenic compound called "Paris Green" to control the greedy Colorado potato beetle, which was spreading eastward. By 1900, arsenic was used so widely in the United States that it led to the first legislation governing the safe application of agricultural chemicals. Two leading fungicides, chemicals to combat plant fungi, were

The work crew above stacks hay the old-fashioned way with pitchforks and muscle power on a Nebraska farm in 1903. Below, men feed sheaves into a 1920s thresher.

also introduced around this time. One was "Bordeaux Mixture," a combination of copper sulfate and hydrated lime, used to control downy mildew on grapevines. The other was lime sulfur, which helped protect against diseases of fruit trees.

Animal diseases and animal pests also were the object of a concerted attack in mid-nineteenth-century America. Two circumstances prompted this. The first was the discovery in the 1860s that many diseases were caused by microbes, or germs. The second was that veterinary medicine, the care and treatment of animals, was established as a separate branch of medicine. Thereafter, animals were immunized against diseases and given medication if they were sick. A diseased animal was removed from the herd so it wouldn't spread the illness. These methods helped make the rapidly expanding dairy and livestock industries more secure and more profitable.

Displaying the season's bounty, these proud Wisconsin farmers pose for a portrait in 1895. With home canning to help, they ate well all winter.

Protecting the Water Supply

As scientific advances in agriculture became more widespread, protecting the farmer's supply of water also became a major concern. Water was a prime factor in the success or failure of farming in many areas of the arid West. The first irrigation engineering was inaugurated by the Mormons in the late 1840s. They began diverting water from Utah's mountain creeks to its dry valley bottomlands by means of simple ditches. In 1877, Congress passed the Desert Land Act, which encouraged farmers in the Southwest to practice irrigation by offering various land grants as a reward. A few water cooperatives were formed as a result, but they proved to be financial disasters in almost every case. Finally, in 1902, federal and state authorities decided to become directly involved in irrigation projects, and this led to the creation of the Reclamation Service, a federal agency dedicated to improving land and water management. By 1919, the Service had led the way in turning vast areas from the Dakotas, Nebraska, Kansas, Oklahoma, and Texas to the West Coast into some of the most productive land in the country. In all, some nineteen million acres of land were involved.

The Educated Farmer

The success of these advances, some of which were a far cry from traditional farming practices, depended on the ability of farmers to keep up with new developments. Books such as those by Jethro Tull were a start in this process. So too were the voluntary societies for the promotion of better agriculture that began to come into existence in the late 1700s. They tried to keep their members up-to-date with reports on new techniques and labor-saving devices that had been developed at home and abroad. But their members were mostly gentlemen farmers, and their influence was limited.

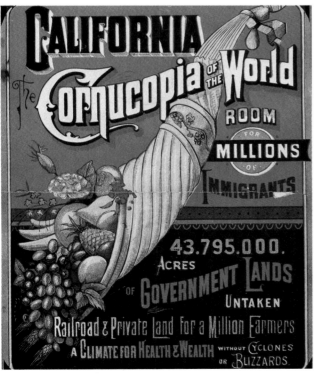

The rich soil of the Midwest made gigantic vegetables like the cabbage above almost commonplace. California could be even more productive, as the nineteenth-century railroad poster, left, promises.

The Plant Wizard

Luther Burbank, "the Plant Wizard," as his contemporaries called him, is credited with developing more than eight hundred new varieties of fruits, vegetables, plants, and flowers.

Born in 1849, Burbank became fascinated by the science of plant breeding when he read the works of Charles Darwin. After graduating from school in Massachusetts, he bought a farm and began testing Darwin's theories of natural selection. By applying the techniques of crossbreeding and hyridization, and by destroying all but the very best examples of each generation, he was able to alter for the better such characteristics as size, color, flavor, and texture in the plants he grew.

Burbank's first commercial success was the Idaho potato. In 1875, he was able to sell the improved variety to a nurseryman, and he used the profits to move his operation to California. There he continued to experiment for another fifty years. Burbank's influence on American farming and the American diet, through his plant introductions and his writings, remains enormous.

Ordinary farmers became better informed when organizations such as the Berkshire Agricultural Society were established. This group began in Massachusetts in 1811 and soon opened branches all over the North. The Society developed a number of techniques for promoting better farm management. Perhaps the most important was the concept of the county fair, which offered farmers competitions and awards for excellence in plowing, crop raising, stock breeding, milk production, egg laying, and various other agricultural pursuits. The first newspapers devoted to farm issues appeared shortly afterward, and they helped spread new ideas and information about new farming techniques to a wider audience.

The next impetus to the advancement of progressive farming was the agricultural college. As early as the 1780s, leading citizens in America had advocated special schools devoted to training farmers. But the first such college did not open until 1823 in Gardiner, Maine. The state of Maine set a precedent by providing some of the money for tuition, in the belief that better farmers would help the country as a whole and were a benefit to society at large.

This became the general policy in the United States some forty years later, when the real growth in agricultural colleges and agricultural research occurred. Two major federal laws, enacted in 1862, made this growth possible. Both were astonishingly advanced and foresighted for the times. The first was the College Land Grant Act, which provided funds for every state in the Union to establish and maintain at least one public college of agriculture and mechanical arts. (Sixty-nine such institutions now exist.) The second law created the United States Department of Agriculture. It was followed in 1887 by the Hatch Act, which provided for the establishment of experimental farms and county extension agents in every state. The agents traveled around each state, providing farmers with the latest agricultural information. These laws set up a network of resources that made it possible for even the smallest farmer in the most distant part of the country to gain knowledge and help in the latest farming techniques.

The Changing Marketplace

Science and technology also began to have an effect on the foods available in the marketplace. The growth of rail transportation, together with the development of refrigerated freight cars in the late 1880s, made possible the economic shipment of fresh meats, vegetables, and fruits from one end of the country to the other. Growth and change in the food-processing industry made other farm products widely available year round. In 1809, the French confectioner Nicolas Appert patented the

The American peanut is a crop of many virtues. Not only is its seed an excellent source of protein and oil, but the plant feeds livestock and enriches soil.

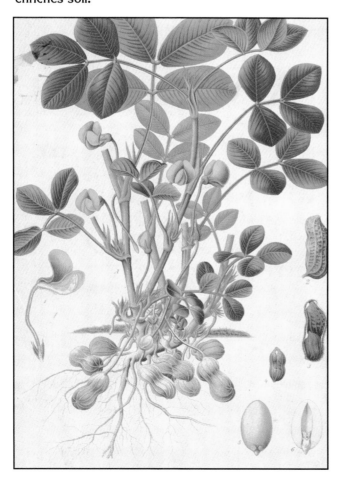

George Washington Carver

The world-renowned botanist and educator George Washington Carver was born in Missouri during the Civil War. The son of slaves, he managed against extraordinary odds to graduate from Iowa State Agricultural College in 1894. From there he went to teach and carry on research at the new Tuskegee Institute in Alabama.

Carver found most farms and farmers in Alabama in a desperate state. He recognized that single-crop cotton farming and bad tillage practices were destroying the region's soil. To reverse the trend, Carver introduced diversified crops such as peanuts and sweet potatoes. There was little commercial market for such crops, so Carver created some three hundred new uses for them. From various parts of the peanut plant, for example, he made imitation cheese, coffee, ink, dyes, and soap.

Carver instituted a "classroom on wheels," which took the message of better farming into distant rural areas. He died in 1943, leaving his entire estate to Tuskegee.

By 1870, some thirty million cans of fruits and vegetables were sold in the United States. In 1910, when the photo at right of tomato canners at work was taken, the government estimated that each American ate some twelve and a half pounds of canned foods a year.

A vast array of canned and packaged foods were available to shoppers in this Sunrise, Wyoming, grocery, photographed around 1900.

first process for preserving sterilized foods in glass jars. But it was not until the American dairyman Gail Borden began canning condensed milk in 1856 that the true potential for marketing canned foods became obvious. By 1870, some thirty million cans of food were sold every year. The industry continued to grow enormously until quick-frozen foods were developed in the 1930s.

The Need for Conservation

The consequences of all these developments in industrializing American agriculture have been dramatic, to say the least. In 1830, it took from 250 to 300 man-hours of plowing, sowing, harvesting, and threshing to produce 100 bushels of wheat. By 1890 this figure had been reduced to 40 to 50 man-hours. Today the crop harvested is of better quality in many ways—it grows faster, remains more resistant to disease, and provides more nutrition.

In the 1904 photograph at left, factory workers clean berries that will be canned.

But the resources used by American farmers to achieve this improvement have grown at an even faster rate. Vast amounts of petrochemicals are used for fuel, fertilizers, and pesticides. And vast amounts of water and topsoil are wasted. David Pimentel, an insect ecologist at Cornell University's College of Agriculture and Life Sciences, has estimated that it takes an average of 2,790 calories of petrochemical energy to produce, harvest, and deliver a can of corn to the consumer. The can of corn itself provides a person with only 270 calories of energy. It seems clear, therefore, that if the United States is to prosper agriculturally in the future, it will have to adopt less wasteful techniques and do so quickly.

Fortunately, as we have noted, some of these techniques are already in use on some commercial farms. Others are being readied for use in the future, as we shall see.

CHAPTER 5

A New World of Plants from the Laboratory

Looking into the future, we can foresee that twenty years from now most of the crops we know today will be grown from plants that have been "improved" or reinvented in some way in a genetics laboratory. Genetics is the scientific study of genes, the units by which characteristics such as size and rate of growth are passed on from one generation to the next.

Some crops will be improved through a technique called gene splicing, in which genes are transplanted from one plant (or animal) to another. In this way characteristics such as resistance to disease can be artificially passed on to improve a crop.

Many other crops will be improved by conventional plant-breeding techniques. But this will be done with a degree of precision and efficiency unimaginable just a few years ago. What used to take breeders many years to achieve—and nature many thousands of years—will be done in months or even weeks! These laboratory crops will be small miracles of applied research. They will be specially bred to grow faster; to ripen at a particular time; to resist disease, drought, or frost; to make better use of sunlight or fertilizers. They will, in short, be just what the farmer ordered.

We can also say that, twenty years from now, Americans will be eating a number of plants unknown in this country today. Some of these plants are already a normal part of people's diets in Asia, Africa, or South America, but have never been tried in the United States. They will become economically important in America because they taste good and are excellent sources of nutrition.

Two African violet leaves are grown in solution, left. The leaf at left is setting profuse roots, thanks to the root-growth hormone NAA.

Supermarket on a Stalk

Among the most exotic plants now being studied as foods for the future, none has created more excitement than the winged bean, a protein-rich, tropical legume that has been called a "supermarket on a stalk." The winged bean is highly nutritious in virtually all its parts. Its fleshy pods taste like green beans, its leaves like spinach, its flowers like mushrooms, and its roots like a potato. The seeds, when pressed, yield an unsaturated oil, and what is left can be milled into a nutritious flour. The winged bean is also a winner in the farmer's field, growing in poor, sandy, or clay soil and supplying all its own fertilizer needs through the bacteria that grow on its roots.

Known for generations as a backyard vegetable in New Guinea and parts of Southeast Asia, the winged bean exists in at least eight hundred native varieties, some of which offer such additional virtues as resistance to drought and disease. Now being experimentally cultivated in some seventy nations, the winged bean's potential usefulness can hardly be overestimated.

Other soon-to-be discovered crops have been overlooked even in their native lands.

In the past, new food crops were discovered and introduced more or less by chance—as a result of trade, war, or human migration. Now trained plant specialists are exploring the earth in search of new and useful foods and fibers.

Both the newly invented and newly discovered plants will fill an urgent need. Agricultural futurists forecast a continuing increase in the world's population, which means that there will be many more mouths to feed. Merle Jensen, of the University of Arizona's Environmental Research Laboratory, predicts that the world population will increase by 50 percent over the next twenty years, reaching a level of six billion. Other futurists estimate that this figure will not be reached until 2025. In any event, to put this figure in perspective, consider that world population reached the one-billion mark in 1850, doubled to two billion in 1930, and doubled again to four billion by 1975.

Plant Diversity to Fight Disease

The need for more food in the future is not the only reason scientists and agricultural technologists are attempting to reverse one current trend —toward growing a decreasing number of crops of just a few genetic varieties of plants. They favor, instead, a type of agriculture in which many different kinds of crops are grown from a much wider genetic pool of plants. This goal is based on the idea that plant diversity and genetic variety provide the greatest protection against worldwide epidemics of plant diseases and attacks by insects.

Pathogens, specific causes of disease, such as bacteria, viruses, fungi, and insects, are not new, of course. They have been around since there have been "hosts" (plants, animals, or humans) to support them. But the damage they could do in the past was limited by certain conditions that went along with small-scale farming. Perhaps the most important was the need for a farmer to be

Representative of today's large-scale single-crop farms is the Montana wheat farm at right. A line of tractors crosses the "amber waves of grain."

self-sufficient, or nearly so. Farmers typically planted small plots of many different crops alongside each other. There might be vegetables, grains, fruits, plants that supplied animal feed, and plants for dyes and fibers and medicinal purposes. This created effective barriers of space against the transmission of pathogens, which typically travel best when potential host plants are close together *(see Glossary, Pathogen).*

Small farmers also used to rotate their crops. They planted different crops in succeeding years or left the earth fallow for a time. As a result, a pathogen that took up residence with one season's crop would winter over in the soil only to find itself without a natural host in that location the next season. Farmers normally gathered their own seeds and root stocks from plant varieties growing locally. This kept in existence countless commu-

nities of plants that were genetically different from each other. Pathogens tend to adapt themselves to the particular weaknesses of their host. They were therefore less able to thrive in the next valley, where they found plants of somewhat different genetic parentage. Because of this, diseases tended to move slowly and peter out before they traveled very far. (It should be noted, however, that even with greater genetic diversity farmers in the past lost a large percentage of their crops to pests of various kinds.)

In contrast, today's agricultural practices have created conditions that are favorable to the spread of pathogens. As their farms have become more and more mechanized, farmers have tended to abandon mixed farming in favor of growing one large crop. The crop chosen is likely to be one of just twenty species that make up the bulk of the

Corn has been dramatically improved by plant breeders in this century. At left is the maize grown by the Indians. A variety cultivated in 1900, "the best yellow corn in the world" at the time, is shown below. But new hybrids, introduced in the 1930s, quickly raised corn yields from an average of 40 bushels per acre to 100 or even 120. At right is a variety popular with today's gardeners.

world's plant foods. The crop is probably grown on a huge tract of land. Fields of wheat may stretch without interruption for a hundred miles. Soybeans may occupy thousands of acres. Of the hundreds of varieties of wheat or soybeans that are available to the farmer, the cultivar, or variety the farmer chooses to grow, is probably one of a handful of "superstar" hybrids or crossbreeds. These hybrids have been created by plant breeders in response to farmers' demands for consistent high-yield crops of uniform size, shape, maturity date, color, and the like. *(See Glossary, Hybrid, Mixed Farming, Monoculture.)*

Such specialization carries risks. A classic example is the epidemic that afflicted the U.S. corn crop in 1970. For several decades before this, most of the corn grown in the United States was descended from one of a handful of commercial hybrids. Of these, 80 percent had one parent in common—a variety of corn called "Texas male sterile." Then along came a fungus called *Helmin-*

thosporium maydis, which causes corn-leaf blight. The fungus had been around for decades, apparently doing little harm. But in 1970 it produced a particularly harmful strain. In an unusually moist growing season, this strain attacked the nearly uniform host of corn plants and produced a disaster for corn growers. Fifteen percent of the entire crop was lost to the disease, and in some states the level reached 50 percent. Only the onset of drier weather prevented greater damage.

Although it was a financial disaster, the 1970 corn blight provided a useful lesson. Farmers became aware that in the process of achieving a uniformly high-yield, low-cost crop, they had sacrificed the greater security that came with agricultural diversity.

Even as the blight was doing its terrible damage, breeders of commercial seed corn were working on the problem. They devised a number of new corn varieties whose genetic makeup endowed them with a resistance to the leaf-blight

fungus. No similar epidemics have occurred to the corn harvest since then. Plant breeders specializing in other major crops took heed, as well. Most began introducing new genetic material to their high-yield hybrids on a regular basis. This, they hoped, would provide protection against pathogens as they evolved.

Breeding Improved Plants

Breeding resistance to disease into a particular plant variety is just one of the many goals of the plant breeder. Scientists took over the job of improving plants from farmers at the beginning of this century. Since then, commercial seed companies have been the farmers' main source of seeds. Plant breeding has two basic objectives: to produce plants that provide better yields and better quality.

Raising a plant's resistance to a particular pathogen can result in improved yield. So too can larger and more numerous seeds, fruits, tubers, or

pods; faster growth; and improved performance under various environmental conditions.

Breeders define improved quality as any adaptation that makes a plant better suited to its particular use. Improvement in quality, then, can include many different characteristics. For fruits, it can refer to color, smell, taste, and storageability. For sugar beets and sugarcane, it can mean sugar content. For wheat and other grains it can mean protein content. For certain vegetables and fruits, it can refer to their characteristics when they are either frozen or canned. In the case of fragile produce, such as lettuce, it can refer to transportability and shelf life. And in fiber plants, such as cotton, it can mean fiber length, strength, and fineness.

How do plant breeders normally achieve such improvements? They do it by crossbreeding, or mating, certain parent plants, which are chosen because they have one or more desired characteristics. The breeder hopes the desired traits of each will combine in one or more of the offspring. (See "Hybrids and the Green Revolution," page 71.) This process has been called "compressed evolution," as opposed to the way plants normally develop, or evolve, in nature. In pursuing this process, breeders need a thorough knowledge of the theory of genetic inheritance. They must then recognize the tiniest changes in plants from one generation to the next as they proceed to select and crossbreed varieties that eventually will produce a plant with the desired characteristics. *(See Glossary, Crossbreeding.)*

It's a tricky job, to say the least. As many as one hundred thousand genes may be squeezed into a single plant variety. Moreover, desirable traits are less likely to come from a single gene than from the effects of several genes working together. The breeder may need to make hundreds of crossbreeding operations and thousands of decisions to save some offspring and discard others. It may take a breeder six to twelve years of work to come up with a variety that is able to produce uniform results in his clients' fields.

Even when the new strain finally reaches the production stage at the seed house, the breeder's job is not finished. Continuing changes in the environment, continuing advances in farm technol-

Mendel's original pea plants

First crossbred generation

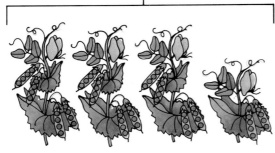

Second crossbred generation

Gregor Mendel: Man of Breeding

The modern science of plant breeding began little more than a century ago at a monastery in Czechoslovakia. An Augustinian monk, Gregor Johann Mendel, became curious about the ways in which plant traits varied from one generation to the next. He set out to perform a series of breeding experiments that he hoped would reveal how and why certain traits appeared in one plant and not in another.

Beginning about 1857, Mendel began the painstaking process of crossbreeding tall pea plants with short ones. In these experiments he transferred the pollen of consistently tall plants to the stamen of shorter plants (top row, in the diagram above). Mendel reasoned that if the resulting seeds produced pea plants of medium height, this would

confirm the theory that was widely held at the time—that the inheritable traits of parents tended to blend in their offspring. According to that theory, a tall and a short plant would produce an offspring of medium height. But Mendel's first generation of pea plants (middle row) all grew tall. The next year he used only his tall hybrid plants for breeding. The results were startling. Although tallness predominated in the next generation (bottom row), about one in four plants turned out to be short. This indicated that the trait for shortness had somehow survived. Mendel called the trait for tallness **dominant** *and the trait for shortness* **recessive**.

In 1865, Mendel announced the results from these and other experiments, but scientists ignored him. Not until 1900 did other scientists confirm his findings.

Mendel's theories can be summarized in three basic concepts:

1. Every living thing is made up of pairs of inherited units (genes) governing every characteristic from size to color, with each parent contributing half of each pair of units.

2. In each pair of units, one unit will usually dominate its partner, as tallness triumphed over shortness in Mendel's experiments.

3. Characteristics determined by individual genes may be transmitted to offspring independent of one another. They may also combine in many variations—one pea plant may be tall with smooth, green peas, whereas another tall plant of the same generation may have wrinkled, yellow peas.

Mendel did not understand the scientific basis for his discoveries. But by the 1940s scientists had identified the precise physical materials of inheritance that Mendel's work reflected—genes and chromosomes. They had also learned to manipulate them in crossbreeding programs that produced markedly better strains of plants for farmers.

ogy, and continuing adaptations by pathogens all contribute to shortening the useful life span of most commercial hybrids to seven to nine years.

The Power of Primitive Varieties

For this reason, breeders must return again and again to a plant species' gene pool for material from which to construct new hybrids. This brings us back to the need for greater diversity in the world's agricultural production. The traditional source of much of this genetic raw material is contained in more primitive varieties of domesticated plants that have evolved over many years through natural selection—and in their relatives that have grown in the wild. These more primitive strains of plants are called "land races." Over hundreds of generations, geographically separate communities of these land races have developed all kinds of adaptations to their different—and sometimes harsh—environments. Because of this, they may contain unique genetic material, which could be extremely useful in the future, when marginal lands, such as deserts, will have to be farmed. *(See Glossary, Land Races.)*

The surviving land races and other primitive plant varieties are found mainly in their places of origin. Generally these are lonely, mountainous regions of the Mediterranean, the Near East, North Africa, China, India, and Central and South America. There, until recently, the plant ecology of the land went undisturbed. Many of these areas are now changing rapidly. Economic progress and population growth are taking place. Their farmers are now using the high-yield hybrid seeds of Western agriculture. In doing so, they are extinguishing a wealth of unique genetic resources that can never be replaced or recreated in a laboratory. For example, the ancient ancestors of corn were perennials, plants that grew year after year. They might have been of great value to breeders in developing a modern variety of perennial corn, but they have long since disappeared.

A Plant Collection Program

The loss of this vast library of genetic material and information could have a severe impact on the future of agricultural research. For this reason,

a number of government and private organizations have recently set up a program to collect and store the seeds of endangered plant species before it is too late. The International Board for Plant Genetic Resources was established by the United Nations in 1974 to create a network of gene banks around the world.

The largest and probably the most scientifically advanced facility for gene conservation is the National Plant Germplasm System (NPGS), run by the U.S. Department of Agriculture (USDA). The NPGS is made up of a network of agencies that oversees the introduction of new plant materials, collects and preserves old and obsolete plant materials, and provides information to plant breeders and researchers. Regional plant introduction stations of the NPGS are responsible for looking after groups of commercially important crops. The North Central Regional Plant Introduction Station at Ames, Iowa, for example, is the main research-and-development center for alfalfa, sweet clover, beets, tomatoes, and cucumbers.

The regional stations keep working collections of many plant varieties, and these are available to plant breeders and scientists. Their seed-storage facilities are like checking accounts that are added to and drawn upon each day. The NPGS also keeps what is in effect a seed savings account. This is the National Seed Storage Laboratory in Fort Collins, Colorado. Established by the USDA in 1958, the laboratory houses America's permanent collection of seeds. Seeds are submitted by public agencies, including agricultural colleges and research stations, by seed companies, and by plant breeders. The donors provide full details about the seeds' origins, along with other information that might be helpful to future breeders. The seeds are prepared for storage in one of the laboratory's ten fireproof vaults. Usually ten to twenty thousand seeds are required to insure an adequate supply for testing and other purposes.

Before they are stored, the seeds are dried until they contain less than 5 percent moisture. They are then placed in heat-sealed, foil-laminated pouches for cold storage at 0 to −4 degrees Fahrenheit. At this temperature most kinds of seeds keep for more than thirty years. Some seeds are now being frozen at −322 Fahrenheit in liquid nitrogen. Periodically, samples are examined and tested. Occasionally, some are planted and the resulting seeds are harvested and stored for another thirty years.

The Fort Collins lab currently holds 190,000 plant varieties belonging to around 1,200 different plant species. Most of them are major species of food and fiber resources. As many as 11,000 new seeds are added each year.

Conventional plant breeders will continue to make use of genetic materials in the world's seed-storage laboratories. Recently, for instance, U.S. breeders have been trying to develop a resistance in cereal crops to yellow dwarf virus, a major pathogen. They appear to have found the material they need, after what amounted to a search for a genetic needle in a haystack. The material was in a stored collection of primitive barley varieties found only in the Ethiopian highlands.

At the same time, new technologies for improving plants will be used increasingly as the possibilities of recombinant DNA (also known as gene splicing) and plant tissue culture are more fully understood. *(See Glossary, DNA, Gene Splicing.)*

The Role of Gene Splicing

Gene splicing belongs to the science of molecular biology. Like those of animals and humans, the genetic behavior of plants is governed by its DNA (deoxyribonucleic acid), or hereditary code. Gene splicing involves inserting one or more "new" genes into the DNA of a plant. In this way, a new and desirable characteristic associated with that gene is implanted. Unlike normal breeding techniques, gene splicing makes it possible to transplant genes from one species of plant to another. In theory, it is also possible to transplant genes from the animal kingdom to the vegetable kingdom.

In the technology of gene splicing, a plant is chosen for some special desirable characteristic, such as lush color. Then the nucleus of a single cell is isolated from the plant. The specific gene responsible for the color or other desired characteristic is then pinpointed in the nucleus. The strand of DNA is broken at this place and the gene

removed. The gene fragment is then copied countless times by placing it in a bacterial medium, where it multiplies quickly. The copies, or clones, of the genes are then inserted into the nuclei of cells taken from other plants the genetic engineer wants to improve.

Up to now, no actual living plant has been achieved by this kind of gene transfer. For one thing, the specific functions of most genes have not yet been identified. Selecting and splicing particular genes to gain desired results is not always possible. But gene splicing moved several steps closer to becoming a practical reality in 1981 when the "sunbean" was conceived. The sunbean is a mixture of the French bean and the sunflower plant. Two researchers, John Kemp of the USDA's Agricultural Research Service and Timothy C. Hall, professor of horticulture at the University of Wisconsin at Madison's College of Agriculture and Life Sciences, succeeded in inserting the gene for protein production from a French bean into the genetic code of a sunflower cell. They did this with the help of a bacterium that causes a disease called crown gall. When the bacteria were introduced to the cells of sunflowers, one of the crown gall's natural hosts, the genetic instructions for making bean protein went along with them. The instructions then became a permanent part of the sunflower's DNA.

So far no sunbean plant has been raised from these altered cells. Scientists first need to discover more about the way certain genes in an organism's genetic code are turned on or off. But the fact that it will one day be possible to create a sunflower that makes protein now seems assured.

Meanwhile, bioengineers are working on several top-priority projects. One is the creation of crops that will absorb and use artificial fertilizers more efficiently. Another is the engineering of plants that will be able to make their own nitrogen fertilizers, as leguminous plants like peas, clover, and alfalfa do now. A third is the development of high-yield grains such as corn and wheat that will grow perennially. And a fourth is the creation of plants that are more efficient in photosynthesis, since ordinary crops now convert less than 1 percent of available solar energy into plant matter.

Hybrids and the Green Revolution

Since World War II, some of the most interesting work in hybridization has focused on developing hardy, high-yield cereals to meet the nutritional needs of Third World countries. American plant breeder Norman E. Borlaug, above left, won a Nobel Peace Prize in 1970 for his work in developing high-performance wheats that were especially well suited to growth in the semiarid climate and soils of Mexico. Other plant breeders working in the Philippines produced new strains of rice. Farmers using the new hybrids, and related fertilizer and water programs, achieved yields that were on average 35 percent greater than those using traditional seeds.

These spectacular increases in production were hailed as a "Green Revolution" when the hybrids were introduced in other Third World countries. Unfortunately, the rising price of petroleum-based fertilizers has resulted in a severe cutback of production levels. The new wheat and rice hybrids have also proven to be vulnerable to diseases that attack plants. But breeders believe that these hurdles can be overcome if sufficient research money is available.

Another major achievement of breeders using conventional crossbreeding techniques to produce hybrids is the development of triticale, upper right, a food crop that tastes like mild rye and is highly resistant to disease. Triticale is the first successful mating of two plant species, wheat (triticum in Latin) and rye (secale). Under development currently at the University of Manitoba in Canada and at Mexico's International Wheat Improvement Center, this new hybrid has produced yields 50 percent higher than wheat yields. Perhaps of even greater long-term consequence, triticale offers superior nutritional value; it has a high level of lysine, an essential amino acid rarely found in cereal grains.

Like many other new foods, triticale has met with slow acceptance in the United States. But it is expected to play a leading role in the Green Revolution, particularly in parts of the world where wheat does not grow well. At the very least, it is a model of the new kinds of plants with highly desirable traits that can be achieved by crossbreeding.

Natural Selection Through Tissue Culture

Tissue culture is also a relatively new technology. It does not offer the plant geneticist the possibility of making as wide a range of radical plant alterations. But its simplicity and efficiency are just as important to the future of agriculture as gene splicing. Tissue culture, sometimes called "compressed evolution," is an artificial way of speeding up a plant species' natural tendency to change, or evolve, in response to environmental conditions. Using tissue culture, scientists attempt to isolate plant varieties that are tailored to thrive in a specific environment and then to clone them by the millions. *(See Glossary, Cloning, Tissue Culture.)*

Tissue culture begins with a plant geneticist first placing a tiny piece of the plant, usually a bit of leaf tissue, in a laboratory tube containing a special growth medium. The geneticist then exposes it to proper temperature and light conditions. (Sometimes the geneticist will include a chemical that increases the likelihood that genes will undergo spontaneous changes.) In a matter of days, the tissue cells multiply, forming a clump or "callus" of as many as forty million cells. The tube is then placed in a machine that shakes it and causes the callus to break down into single cells. The cells are then placed in other laboratory tubes and exposed to various environmental conditions.

For example, the geneticist may be looking for a type of wheat that can grow in a mildly salty soil. He will add an appropriate amount of salt to the cell solution. The geneticist may be looking for a plant variety that adapts well to hot temperatures. In this case, the tube will be placed in a climate-controlled cabinet regulated to the desired temperature.

A process that is very much like the process of natural selection in nature then occurs. But nature can take thousands of years to produce new adaptations. Tissue culture methods produce them in months or days. The test conditions are too harsh for about 98 percent of the cells, and they

Workers at the National Seed Storage Laboratory conduct live seed germination tests to find out how well various seeds will survive over long periods.

die almost at once. About 2 percent survive, however. These survivors are mutants, cells that differ from the norm. They have developed some factor in their genetic makeup that allows them to withstand the new challenge they face.

The same procedure may be repeated several times. Eventually, the plant geneticist is satisfied that he has sifted out the one-in-ten million mutant that is best able to tolerate the particular environmental conditions he is breeding for. At this point, the geneticist separates the cells once more. Then the geneticist introduces hormones that speed the formation of roots and shoots, and awaits the birth of a generation of tiny plantlets. When the plantlets are large enough for handling, they are set out in a greenhouse. Eventually, the plants produce seeds of their own. From these seeds are grown the first generation of the new specially adapted variety.

Tailoring Plants for Specific Purposes

The basic techniques for plant tissue culture have been around for many years. It is only now that they are beginning to be applied in the breeding of plants for agriculture. Murray W. Nabors of Colorado State University, one of the pioneers of this kind of genetic engineering, thinks future lab-

Several billion seeds, covering almost a hundred thousand varieties of plants, are kept at the National Seed Storage Laboratory at Fort Collins, Colorado.

oratories might design varieties to suit the needs of growers in specific areas of the world. Nabors cites as an example a group of farmers in India who might want to introduce corn into a new area with a known water supply, known temperature extremes, and so forth. "Samples of the [corn] plant or its seed would be sent to the laboratory, and for a standard fee the lab would develop a line of corn tailored to the environment of that area."

Nabors is particularly excited about the possibility of creating plant varieties that are resistant to drought or salt. These would be suited to the growing conditions of dry, sun-drenched parts of Mexico, Pakistan, India, and the Middle East. Why salt resistant? Because continuous irrigation of land, accompanied by rapid evaporation, causes the tiny particles of salt in the water gradually to accumulate and reach levels that are poisonous to plant growth in some areas. Nabors suggests that "it is cheaper, more economical, and in the long run, smarter to modify the plant to suit the environment than it is to modify the environment to suit the plant."

In his first tissue culture experiments with oats and wheat, Nabors was able to grow cell cultures that would tolerate up to five times the normal salt levels in the soil. Although these changes are exciting in themselves, he thinks they may be only the beginning. Research is now under way at several centers to develop varieties of grain that will flourish either in pure saltwater, or in mixes of 50 percent salt and 50 percent freshwater. This would open up to farming millions of acres of coastal lands washed by salty water.

Tissue culture is obviously a rapid and economical way to develop specially adapted plants. But it also has important possibilities for cloning plants that are bred in the normal way. Date palm trees for starting up orchards or for replacing old, damaged, or dead trees, for example, are usually grown from the offshoots of healthy date palms. But it takes years for a tree to send up even a few

An apple tree, nurtured from selected USDA tissue culture, has begun to differentiate into roots and shoots.

shoots, which means that such new material is hard to come by and costly to the grower. Plant researchers at California's U.S. Date and Citrus Station have now found a way more or less to mass-produce date palm trees by tissue culture. The California scientists believe they will be able to reduce by twenty-five years the time once needed to increase a new variety to five thousand healthy seedlings—and they can do this on one hundred acres less land.

The Possibilities of Growth Regulators

The new genetic technologies have probably received the most attention. But another approach to plant improvement—the development of plant growth regulators—has attracted more research money. Plant growth regulators are the artificially produced chemical equivalents of the natural substances called hormones. Hormones trigger many different mechanisms within a plant. In general,

A plant geneticist at the USDA's experimental station in Beltsville, Maryland, clones peach trees with growth characteristics tailored to high-density orchards.

Scientists have succeeded in transferring a bean gene to sunflower tissue culture. Above, a sunflower plant is injected with the bean's protein gene.

A new hybrid tobacco plant, created by fusing cells of two species, undergoes its initial cell division.

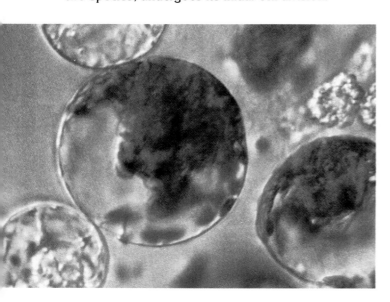

they control the timing and progression of a plant's potential for growth, development, and reproduction.

Scientists first discovered the existence of plant hormones in the 1920s. But it took a number of years to grasp their many functions. It took still more years before they tried to create artificial hormones to change plant performance. Growth regulators turn out to have highly specific effects on different plants. What works with one variety of a species may have little effect on another, even at very high doses. Effective timing and methods of application may vary widely between plants, too, so research is slow and has to be done on a case-by-case basis.

Nevertheless, a number of artificial growth regulators are already being used in commercial farming. They help farmers to realize the greatest potential from the crops they plant. A good example is a hormone called ethylene, known as "nature's ripening agent." Laboratory-created ethylene in liquid form is sprayed on pineapple plants to speed up flowering. This cuts exactly in half the time needed for mature fruits to form—from thirty-six months to eighteen months. Ethylene is also used to produce uniform ripening of a fruit, so that a mechanical harvester only has to pass over a field once to gather an entire crop.

When a growth regulator is applied to sugarcane it increases the size and sugar content of cane stalks. It also makes the cane mature earlier and slows down seed formation. All of these effects contribute to a more bountiful harvest. Ethylene sprayed on apple orchards spurs young trees to flower more profusely so they become ready to bear fruit one or two years earlier than normal. When sprayed on mature trees, ethylene promotes uniform ripening and red coloration. It also loosens the apples from the tree so that the mechanical tree shakers easily harvest them.

More recently, plant growth regulators have been used on large acreages of cereal crops. Grain growers have lost money because of the

Cloned plantlets are grown in test tubes (right), where their varied growth habits can be compared.

problems known as "lodging" and "necking." Lodging is the collapse of lush, top-heavy grasses before they can be gathered. Necking is the tendency of fat, ripe grains to break off just below the head and fall to the ground.

Ironically, both problems are caused by better farming methods—the use of more fertilizer and improved water supplies—which have made cereals such as wheat and barley grow almost too well in temperate parts of the United States and Europe. An ethylene-type regulator is now used to shorten and strengthen the straw without reducing the growth of the grain. For farmers the result is faster, cleaner harvests: in some cases, 25 to 40 percent more bushels of grain have been harvested per acre.

Thomas Jefferson once said: "The greatest service which can be rendered any country is to add a useful plant to its culture." Our third president would be astonished to see the wonders that are now being performed to expand the world of useful agricultural plants and make them more vigorous. Although there is still not enough nutritious food to feed everyone in the world, the plants and plant technologies needed to achieve that goal seem to be within reach.

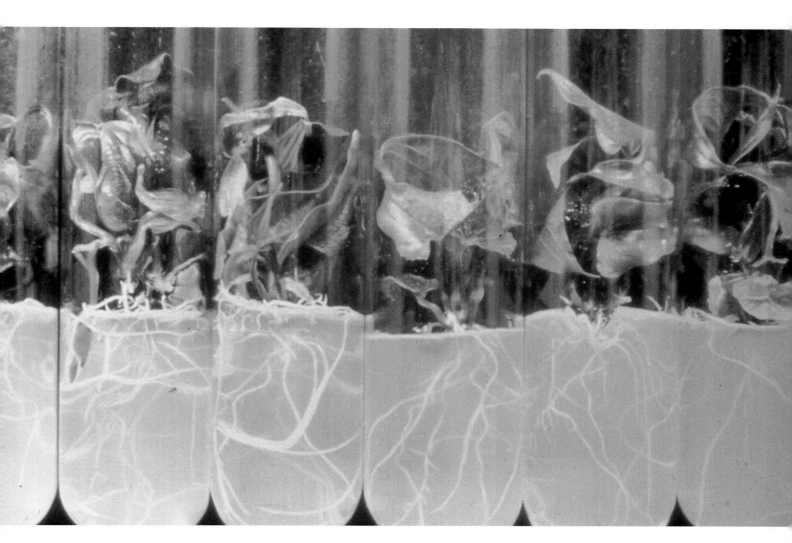

CHAPTER 6

Science and Technology Change the Face of Farming

"You see this greenhouse? It covers a little less than two-thirds of an acre, but in that space we can raise as much lettuce in a year's time as an open-field farmer on thirty to forty acres. And we can do it in all seasons, with fewer helpers, fewer risks, no pesticides, and a consistently high quality of produce in the bargain."

G. Graham Davidson, president and founder of Agrownautics Inc., speaks with understandable pride of his small, highly specialized agricultural factory in northwestern Connecticut. With the help of just three full-time growers and a modest collection of equipment that seems anything but high-tech, each week he harvests as many as fifteen thousand heads of a bibb-type lettuce called *ostinata*. Hours later the leafy, emerald green lettuce has been delivered to grocers' cases as far as a hundred miles away, and it looks and tastes as fresh as if it had been raised in the customer's own backyards.

Agricultural experts predict that in the near future farms such as this one, engaging in high-density indoor farming, will become much more commonplace for growing certain specialty crops.

This kind of farming is known as Controlled Environment Agriculture (CEA), the general term for a variety of advanced growing systems. Using these systems, farmers raise crops in large greenhouses or in other sheltered environments where light, temperature, air movement, water, fertilizers, pests, and various other factors are all carefully controlled to enable plants to achieve the greatest possible growth.

Center-pivot irrigation, a sprinkler system that moves in a circle, distributes water evenly and produces lush, uniformly colored fields such as these.

G. Graham Davidson, one of the owners of a CEA farm in Connecticut, makes a routine inspection of his abundant lettuce crop, which is harvested daily all year round.

Depending on the climate, latitude, and supply of sunlight, plants in CEA facilities may be grown under glass, fiberglass, or plastic enclosures that admit the sun's rays. Or the plants may be grown in windowless buildings where overhead "grow-lights" provide a controlled amount of artificial sunlight. Old warehouses and abandoned industrial buildings have also been converted into food factories.

Virtually all CEA buildings use "hydroponics," or water cultivation. In this technique, all the necessary nutrients, including nitrogen, phosphorus, potassium, calcium, magnesium, manganese, sulfur, iron, boron, molybdenum, zinc, copper, and chloride, are carefully measured and fed to the plants in a hydroponic solution. The water circulates within a closed system and is endlessly filtered and recycled. In this way, both the water and the nutrients are used at close to 100 percent efficiency. Sometimes the plants are supported in screens that float on top of shallow tanks of hydroponic solution, with their roots submerged. In other cases, they are supported in styrofoam, vermiculite, or sterilized sand, and buried irrigation tubes trickle water to their roots. (See Glossary, Hydroponics.)

Climate-control systems automatically clean the air and keep the temperature within a certain range. Lettuce grows best at a temperature of from 76 to 78 degrees Fahrenheit, for example. Carbon dioxide, normally present in the air at approximately three hundred parts per million, may be increased to one thousand parts or more per million. This improves photosynthesis and the building of plant tissue.

Pests are not usually a problem because of the hospitallike sanitary conditions. In some CEA operations, workers even wear sterilized uniforms and footgear to reduce the chance of bringing in soil-borne plant pathogens from the outside.

Davidson believes CEA technology was fortunate to come of age about the time people became conscious of health and good nutrition. "There was an instant market for superfresh, additive-free products like the kind of lettuce we grow," he says.

But, Davidson points out, there are still some obstacles to the widespread development of indoor food factories, particularly in colder climates. One is cost. Any plant can be grown better and faster under such protected conditions. But at present the cost is too high for most crops in the United States, either because the space needed is too large compared to the yield or because the growing period is too long.

The lettuce Davidson grows can be produced at a competitive price for several reasons. "It has little or no waste," he notes. "You eat everything but the roots. It grows from seed to harvest in six to seven weeks. It requires little handling at any stage of growth. And consumers who value its freshness are willing to pay a little more for it, which makes it competitive, at a slightly higher price, with lettuce that has had to travel seven to ten days from West Coast farms."

Davidson and other advocates of CEA farming expect that more kinds of vegetables, including tomatoes, cucumbers, spinach, herbs, and the like, will ultimately be grown on CEA farms, particularly around large urban areas. They see this happening as the cost of conventional farming and long-distance transportation of food rises in the United States.

The Spread of CEA Farming

Outside the United States, crop raising in CEA structures is already taking place in many countries. The number of acres given over to growing food indoors has been increasing by as much as 10 percent a year. CEA has become particularly popular in areas where prime farmland and water for irrigation are in short supply, or where the climate is too dry, too hot, or too cold to support a productive growing season in the field.

Abu Dhabi, a coastal desert state on the Persian Gulf, is an excellent example of a country in which CEA farming is a boon. It has an annual rainfall of only two to three inches a year. Previously the expanding population depended on imports and on the small surplus of crops grown at the country's single oasis. Now CEA buildings produce a ton of fresh vegetables each day for a steadily increasing population.

Abu Dhabi's CEA facilities were designed and installed by the University of Arizona's Environmental Research Laboratories. In CEA greenhouses that stretch over five acres, Arab technicians have achieved impressive yields raising cabbages, cucumbers, eggplant, lettuce, okra, peppers, radishes, tomatoes, and turnips. They have harvested as much as three times the poundage of tomatoes and lettuce, five times the poundage of cabbage and okra, and twelve times the poundage of cucumbers and eggplant as average open farm fields in the United States, when the square footage of space is compared.

Another promising use of CEA is under way in Canada. Here farmland is limited—only about 5 percent of the land is arable, and in many places the climate is too harsh for farming. In an experimental program, horticulturists at Laurentian University of Sudbury in Ontario are growing vegetables more than a mile underground in the unused galleries of a working nickel mine. Sodium vapor lamps provide fourteen hours of artificial sunlight per day. At 4,000 to 4,600 feet down, temperatures hover around 70 degrees Fahrenheit, which is good for growing tomatoes. At 5,600 feet down, temperatures rise to 78 degrees Fahrenheit, and cucumbers and lettuce grow vigorously at this level.

Under these unusual conditions, and without the benefit of sophisticated CEA equipment, the university's horticulturists are producing one-half to three-quarters of what they would normally harvest in a favorable aboveground environment. Moreover, there are no costs for building maintenance, heating, or cooling. Joseph Shorthouse, the project's director, thinks that once scientists have ironed out the problems, underground gardens of this kind will be of great value, particularly in the remote mining villages of Canada's far

At Puerto Penasco, Mexico, above, the University of Arizona's Environmental Research Laboratory grows crops in a coastal desert setting. A similar program, also conducted by the ERL, is shown below in Abu Dhabi on the Persian Gulf.

One of the many installations that have turned Israel's Negev Desert into productive agricultural land is this closed-system greenhouse, which uses solar and artificial light to keep plants growing day and night. The lush garden shown below was planted at a depth of four thousand feet in an unused mine in Sudbury, Ontario.

north. At present, nearly all food supplies must be flown into these villages at great expense.

As promising as controlled environment agriculture is, it should be noted that it is capable of making only a small contribution to increasing the total yield of world food production. Even so, controlled environment agriculture is typical of the innovative new methods that agricultural scientists and technologists are devising to make farming more efficient and more productive. They are, as we shall see, working on numerous other advances, including more efficient irrigation techniques, better ways of plowing and cultivating land, and new methods of pest control.

Saving Precious Resources

Foremost among the problems these advances are designed to remedy has been the American farmers' waste of precious resources, particularly

land and water. Nearly all phases of early twentieth-century farming tended toward waste—of water, soil, fuel, fertilizers, pesticides, and space. Resources were thought to be more or less unlimited. Now the emphasis is on conservation, but, as the new breed of farmers are proving, conservation that allows for continued high productivity.

The first and most pressing need in the United States is better water management. The U.S. Water Resources Council points out that almost every region west of the Mississippi River has too little water from all sources—precipitation, rivers and lakes, and underground water sources—to continue agricultural production in the usual way, let alone expand it. Conventional methods of farm irrigation must therefore be changed.

The irrigation problems farmers now face arise from their past experience. The Newlands Reclamation Act, passed in 1902, authorized the construction of irrigation projects in sixteen western states. Ever since, under its provisions, federal and state governments have subsidized the construction of new water projects. The price farmers paid for their ongoing supply of water was held at an artificially low level that had no practical relationship to the long-term economic costs to the region or the nation. For this reason, farmers had little financial incentive to conserve water, and they farmed accordingly. They plowed in ways that increased water loss through evaporation, for example, and they used open-ditch methods of irrigation, which meant that they lost through evaporation and seepage as much as two-thirds of the water that was supplied to them.

They were also led early on into a false sense of security by their principal sources of irrigation—surface waters that were tapped from rivers, lakes, and man-made reservoirs and delivered by gravity. They could see that these waters were replenished by nature with each new year and assumed they would always have access to such a water supply.

But by the 1930s, most of the lands within easy reach of surface water systems had been brought under cultivation. Farmers then began to develop more remote, more arid lands, and agriculture in the American West entered a new and potentially more damaging phase of water use. Most of the new acreage depended on groundwater, which was pumped up from water sources deep in the earth called aquifers. Withdrawals from these reserves grew rapidly, much as they had from the surface water sources.

The major difference was that the groundwater supplies were essentially not renewable. For example, the vast Ogallala aquifer supplies water to the states of South Dakota, Nebraska, Colorado, Kansas, Oklahoma, New Mexico, and Texas. Some sections of it are currently being used up at a rate fourteen times faster than they are being replenished. In parts of Oklahoma, the best hope is that the water supply will last another twenty years. In virtually all parts of the huge western farming region, stretching from Nebraska to eastern New Mexico and from Colorado to the Texas Panhandle, it is now necessary for farmers to pump water from ever deeper levels at ever increasing cost.

Advanced Methods of Irrigation

Fortunately, much is now being done to reverse the years of water waste and to bring about sensible methods of conservation. Center-pivot irrigation is one technique that has gained widespread use, as anyone can attest who has flown over the telltale circles of crops that now cover many parts of the West. Twice as efficient in its water use as traditional open ditch irrigation, this system uses a gigantic rotating overhead sprinkler.

Typically, the device consists of a single rotor, or sprinkler, attached at the center of the field to a stationary post. The sprinkler is propelled around the circle of the field on a motorized carriage. The water is sent up from an underground well or some other source through the centerpost and is sprinkled through thousands of tiny holes to fall like rain on the growing plants as the rotor slowly travels around the circular field. The largest center-pivot sprinklers are as much as a quarter of a mile long, and they are capable of watering as many as 125 acres at a time.

A more advanced but more costly method of field irrigation is the trickle-drip system, which was first used on a large scale in Israel's thirsty Negev Desert. This system delivers water—as well as fer-

The search for new CEA technologies to reduce water and heat loss is never ending. Above, tomatoes grow in small cubes that are set atop horticultural rock wool. The porous rock wool, suffused with nutrient water, slows down evaporation markedly. At left, lettuce plants grow bare-rooted in troughs whose water is constantly recycled. Below, soapsuds are used to insulate the double-layer roof of a greenhouse, preventing heat loss in cold climates and sun damage in hot regions.

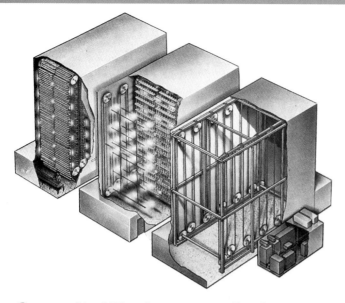

Controlled Environment Agriculture

Controlled Environment Agriculture, or CEA, was first attempted in Rome in the first century A.D., when gardeners of Emperor Tiberius raised cucumbers in a primitive greenhouse. But it was not until after World War II that greenhouse farming was studied scientifically or attempted on a commercial scale.

Today, CEA represents an important share of the food-raising efforts in many technologically advanced countries, with some of the most interesting work being done in such cool-climate, land-limited countries as the Netherlands, Denmark, and Japan. The United States, although deeply engaged in CEA at a research level, has as yet few commercially run CEA installations, primarily because the cost of crops is too high to be competitive in most circumstances.

The most widespread type of CEA is hydroponics, the technique of growing plants in solutions of water and fertilizers. This is almost always done in tightly enclosed structures in which air movement, water, humidity, temperature, and pest control can be kept at near perfect conditions. Sometimes sterile soil substitutes such as sand, gravel, vermiculite, or peat moss are used to provide support for the plants' roots.

Coming decades should see increased efficiency in hydroponic and other CEA technologies. And if predictions of changing worldwide weather conditions prove true, CEA may play a major role in filling the need for food in the future.

The technologies of automated factory production are being wedded to the science of hydroponic agriculture to create indoor food factories that require little human labor. The drawing at top left shows an experimental Austrian system. Two vertical conveyor belts move plants through a structure featuring artificial light and highly reflective surfaces to maximize growing effects. At top right, lettuce is grown on belts that can be reeled in for harvesting and replanting. Above, rigid foam is used as the plant support system. Lightweight boards lift out for easy harvesting.

tilizers and other materials—to the plants' roots through perforated plastic tubing that runs beneath each row of crops. The size of the holes is tailored to the particular plants' capacity to absorb water. Only amounts that can be absorbed trickle out. In theory, at least, water efficiency approaches 100 percent. Trickle-drip irrigation is also more efficient in terms of space. Unlike open-ditch irrigation, which can use many acres of prime farmland for its own conduits, trickle-drip tubes do not take up any field space.

Green fields adjacent to barren desert in the photograph at left, taken in California, graphically show how irrigation has changed the American West.

Perhaps the most impressive technology for conserving water in irrigation is that used in advanced rice farming. It involves the terracing of hundreds of acres of paddies to uniform grades of 0.01 percent. This extraordinary feat of earth sculpturing is used today by California rice growers. It insures an optimum flooding depth during the growing season and facilitates drainage and reuse of as much as two-thirds of the water used. The incredibly accurate terracing is accomplished by means of a laser beam mounted on a tripod in the field. The laser centers on photoelectric cells atop a tractor-drawn land leveler. Signals indicating tiny changes in terrain are communicated to a computer, which operates an electric motor that raises and lowers a scraper blade. The blade levels each paddy to the desired grade.

A New Emphasis on Soil Conservation

Soil is another resource that, like water, has been wasted in the past. It has often been said that a thin layer of topsoil is all that stands between humankind and starvation. This may be something of an exaggeration, but certainly the soil that constitutes the nation's prime farmland must be regarded as a resource to be conserved. It takes longer to replenish soil, once lost, than water and, in fact, topsoil takes centuries to create.

Unfortunately, the very abundance of arable land in the United States, much of it blessed with unusually deep topsoil, has led farmers over the years to violate traditional conservation practices in order to achieve high yields and profits. Crop rotation and fallowing, for example, seemed unnecessary to American farmers when they could readily substitute artificial fertilizers for the decomposed organic matter or humus generated by rotation and fallowing.

Depleted soils can be made to produce bumper crops year after year with ever increasing doses of fertilizer and irrigation. But the cost is high. Depleted soil does not retain water as organically rich

soil does. It is more likely to become compacted and impenetrable. And it is far more subject to erosion by wind.

Besides wasting soil and water, American farmers tended to abandon other conservation methods as well. One reason for this was that they had huge, efficient machines for plowing, seeding, cultivating, and harvesting. In using this machinery farmers often took shortcuts that damaged the land. They stopped contour plowing and terracing. They cut down natural windbreaks. They planted crops "from fence to fence." They used marginal lands that were best left in pasture or wild scrub. They often cultivated crops in continuous rows, even on rolling terrain. And they carefully cleared away all the postharvest stubble whose roots held the soil, aerated it, and reenriched it. These methods created endless vistas of beautifully manicured but highly vulnerable farmland.

The terrible "Dust Bowl" crisis that wracked the Great Plains in the mid-1930s gave Americans their first taste of what soil mismanagement could lead to. Farmers then adopted some soil- and water-conservation practices, but these were not enough. And as technological advances continued and productivity went on rising, many of the lessons of the 1930s were forgotten.

In 1977, the U.S. Department of Agriculture (USDA) warned that soil erosion had become a major problem in over half of the nation's croplands. A study four years later found that the country's 413 million acres of cropland currently lose 2.82 billion tons of soil per year to water and wind. This loss averages out to 6.8 tons of soil per acre. In the state of Iowa alone, fully half of the rich two-foot-deep topsoil that delighted "sod busters" 150 years ago is gone. If this kind of erosion is allowed to continue, says the USDA, the Midwest's corn yields will probably decrease by 30 percent by the year 2020. The USDA has also predicted that other areas will be totally barren in two hundred years unless major changes are instituted.

New Techniques for Conservation

Agricultural scientists have developed several new techniques in recent years to halt soil erosion and depletion. Grouped under the general head-

---

The irrigation project at left, near Blythe, California, uses water from the Colorado River, which supplies water to seven western states and Mexico.

This automated irrigation system employs lasers, computers, and sensors geared to weather and soil data. It may eventually replace more conventional irrigation systems in large-scale commercial operations. Here a prototype is tested in California tomato fields.

ing of "conservation tillage," they are designed to prepare and maintain the soil for productive farming while altering as little as possible the natural structure and stability of the earth. Many of these new techniques eliminate the use of the plow and harrow in favor of such new farm machinery as chisels, sweeps, weed rods, and middlebreakers. Oddly enough, conservation tillage often makes fields look less well tended, but it represents a great advance in preserving the environment. *(See Glossary, Conservation Tillage.)*

One new technique, "zero till," is designed for areas that have great problems with wind and water erosion, such as sloping land, very arid land, and land that has marginal soil to begin with. In this system, crops of various grasses, especially

winter grazing grasses for livestock, are planted in existing sod, with no plowing beforehand. The dense, wild growth protects the soil while the crop grows. The planting is accomplished by a tractor drawing a specially designed seed drill. The drill cuts narrow slits into which seed and fertilizer are dropped in a single operation. (This is a modern version of the first farmers' methods of planting in unplowed earth with a digging stick.)

Another new technique, "minimal till," calls for plowing and seeding to be done in one operation. This means that heavy machinery passes over the land once, not twice. This technique reduces soil compaction, which makes the earth more vulnerable to water erosion. A third approach, called "trash farming," uses special machinery to stir and loosen the soil but leave straw and other crop stubble on the surface of the fields. In a fourth technique, "ridge planting," the farmer plows and plants in every other row.

Intercropping is yet another conservation technique. In intercropped fields, two or more complementary crops are planted in alternating rows. One crop might be a legume, such as deep-rooted alfalfa. This kind of crop puts nitrogen and organic matter into the soil and breaks up the compacted soil beneath. The other would be a cash crop that requires high levels of nitrogen. The two crops grow at different rates and are harvested separately. This provides a broader defense against soil depletion and erosion.

New Ways to Control Weeds and Pests

Conventional practices in tilling the soil have always included weed control with a hand hoe or a mechanical cultivator. But weeding tends to disrupt topsoil. Conservation tillage substitutes for weeding various modern chemical herbicides that are highly selective in killing unwanted plants while leaving crops unharmed. For example, the herbicide atrazine is used on corn crops. The corn is not affected by atrazine, but it kills any weeds and grasses in the field. *(See Glossary, Herbicides.)*

Herbicides such as these are spin offs of World War II research into the uses of plant growth regulators in chemical warfare. Herbicides were first used in agriculture in 1945. They now play an ever increasing role in U.S. farming. The USDA estimates that by the year 2010 as much as 78 percent of the nation's seven major annual crops— corn, soybeans, sorghum, wheats, oats, barley, and rye—will be produced by using a combination of herbicides and zero-tillage agriculture.

It's no wonder that Sylvan H. Wittwer, Director of the Michigan State University Agricultural Experiment Station and a leading expert in agricultural technology, calls conservation tillage "the most significant technology yet developed" for the control of soil erosion and the conservation of land cover, energy, labor, water, soil fertility, and organic matter.

To insure uniform delivery of irrigated water, fields are "dead-leveled" with a laser-guided scraper. Blades automatically adjust to tolerances of less than an inch.

Weeds are just one pest farmers have to worry about. An awesome variety of enemies, which also includes insects and pathogens, stand ready to attack, damage, or wipe out valuable crops. Pests of various kinds reduce the world's agricultural produce by 30 to 35 percent before harvest. In the United States, where more modern methods of agriculture are used, the loss is smaller, about 20 percent. Still, this is equivalent to devoting 67 million acres a year to feeding pests—a stunning loss.

Farmers as well as agricultural scientists must constantly be on the lookout for new and better ways to manage pests. For a few decades farmers used heavy doses of poisonous chemicals in what has been called "the spray and pray" method of control. But gradually it has become clear that chemicals alone are not the answer. They have already caused considerable damage to the environment and to human health. Moreover, in case after case, the pests they were meant to kill have developed ever higher levels of resistance to their effects. Forward-looking farmers are now beginning to use a more moderate, flexible, and socially responsible approach to the problem of pests.

Integrated Pest Management

The new system seeks to control pests, rather than eliminate them altogether. Chemicals are still used, but their role is greatly reduced. Known as Integrated Pest Management (IPM), the system starts with prevention: the farmer chooses disease-resistant plant varieties for planting wherever possible *(see Glossary, Integrated Pest Management)*. The farmer then relies on early detection and quick responses to prevent pest problems from becoming severe. (The Land exhibit at EPCOT Center has instituted one of the most advanced and efficient programs for Integrated Pest Management now in use in a greenhouse growing system in America.)

Two techniques that conserve water and increase yields are seen at left. On an Israeli kibbutz, strawberries are grown under moisture-preserving plastic (top). In Indonesia, farmers grow rice on terraces; the water flows from level to level.

Integrated Pest Management systems make use of a combination of biological, physical, and chemical controls. The farmer must make careful choices. Various factors must be considered, including the needs of the plants at particular stages of growth; the life cycle of the pest population; the possibility of destroying other helpful predators that may be present; and the costs of various alternatives measured against the destructive potential of the pest. What seems to be the best answer one week may not be as good the next. Sometimes, though not very often, the answer will be to leave well enough alone.

Biological Controls

Biological pest control involves the encouragement of natural predators, parasites, and pathogens to keep more harmful pests in check. Virtually every pest has one or more enemies in nature. By using this fact to advantage, the farmer can go a long way toward keeping pest problems within bounds at a reasonable cost. Only a few pests—perhaps 5 to 10 percent—lack strong natural enemies. These are the ones that become problems to farmers. The goal is to organize natural protection against pests before they are able to destroy a crop.

Using biological controls for specific agricultural purposes is an old idea that got pushed aside in the golden age of chemical insecticides and has lately been rediscovered. Indeed, thousands of years ago the Chinese built bamboo bridges between their citrus trees so insect-eaters, such as caterpillar-eating ants, could more easily find their prey. The USDA got into the biological control business in 1885 when it imported and distributed its first collection of Australian ladybug beetles. The Department did this to save the California orange groves from an insect called cottony-cushion scales, which the ladybug beetles attack. Today the USDA has a special unit known as the Insect Identification and Beneficial Insect Introduction Institute, which studies as many as a third of a million insects and mites each year.

As farmers now realize, the range of hungry helpers ready to assist them in controlling pests varies from toads, birds, snakes, and insectivorous fish in farm ponds to ladybugs, lace wings, and yellow-jacket wasps. Less well known, because of their tiny size and mysterious ways, are microbes, such as viruses and bacteria, which wage germ warfare on their hosts.

Hundreds of microbes that attack insects have been identified. One of them, *Bacillus thuringiensis,* causes disease in well over a hundred insects, including the vegetable-devouring cabbage looper. It was isolated in 1914 and has been used for some time as a partial control for a number of pests. Many more microbes will undoubtedly be identified in the future and made commercially available for use against pests. Still others will probably be developed through genetic engineering.

Another form of biological control is the sterilization of male insects. This is done by gamma radiation. Once sterilized, the males cannot breed new generations and their population is greatly reduced. In some cases, this technique can control an insect population to such a degree that no chemical insecticide need be used.

Pheromones and hormones are still other weapons in the biological bag of tricks. Pheromones are chemicals that are secreted by insects and affect the behavior of other individuals of the same species—signaling them to mate, to flee, to eat, and so on. The pheromone that is the female sex attractant, for example, has been used as "bait" to trap and kill large numbers of males or simply to confuse their mating instincts and thus keep the insect population in check.

Hormones are also organic chemicals. They affect insect development and can be used to stop insects from growing into adults, preventing their regeneration. Practical use of pheromones and hormones on a large scale lies farther in the future, however. At this time there is no way to produce these chemicals artificially in quantity and at a reasonable cost.

Physical Controls

Pests can also be controlled through physical pest management. This kind of control requires a large amount of labor. For this reason, it is more practical in CEA than in field agriculture. There are a number of approaches to physical pest control. One is the use of a portable backpack vacuum cleaner that sucks up insects and other small flying pests from leaves. Another is to sterilize the growing medium, using steam, in order to kill certain resident pathogens between plantings. A third is to place sticky tape around the trunks of certain sturdy plants and trees to catch crawling insects. Among other methods are selective pruning and thinning of diseased plants; destroying crop refuse that might be harboring pests; and monitoring water quality.

For field farming, several techniques are under investigation, but the results are not yet conclusive. Among them are the use of reflective strips, which are placed like mulch around cucumbers, squash, and melons. They confuse aphids and thus help to reduce mosaic diseases, which are caused by a virus and which may result in dwarfed leaves. Among various other new methods now being tested as ways to repel insects are high-intensity lights and sound frequencies and radio and electric fields.

Chemical Controls

Finally, there are chemical pest controls. Much as agricultural futurists would like to imagine a world free of chemical insecticides, few think such a time will actually come. Henry Robitaille, chief horticulturist at The Land exhibit at EPCOT Center, speaks for the majority when he says: "Pest management without the use of chemicals is not a realistic approach to large-scale agriculture or worldwide food production, particularly as the population increases and quality farmland decreases."

But Robitaille believes that Integrated Pest Management will make it possible to apply chemicals at low levels and with a much greater awareness of their effects on other parts of the environment.

One promising way of reducing the amount of chemicals that are used is through better methods of application. Dusting crops from a plane or spraying them on the ground with a highly poisonous insecticide risks injuring plants and beneficial organisms along with the targeted pest. Instead, in some cases, pellets of insecticide can be buried

Male tobacco budworms are lured into a trap (right) by a pheromone. A wind vane aims the trap so that the attractant scent trails downwind for maximum effect.

alongside the seed at planting time. Coated for time-release, the insecticide is absorbed by the plant as it becomes available, and little or no toxic material remains in the soil. Weed control using herbicides can also be managed through trickle-drip irrigation in some situations.

Using Plants as Herbicides

Allelopathy is another exciting area of investigation, particularly for weed control. Allelopathy describes the ability of certain plants to release chemicals into the soil—such as phenols and steroids. These chemicals are poisonous to other plants.

In the past, agricultural scientists noted that some kinds of crop rotation worked less well than others and that certain plants grew poorly, if at all, when grown with certain other crops as their neighbors. Tomatoes, for example, will scarcely survive when planted near black walnut trees. Cucumbers die when planted next to red root pigweed. In some cases, the decaying remains of certain plants suppress the growth of a new generation of their own kind. *(See Glossary, Allelopathy.)*

Scientists are now investigating how and why these reactions occur. Theodore I. Kozlowski, Director of the Biotron research facilities at the University of Wisconsin at Madison, expects that, once the interactions of various plants are better understood, allelopathy will be used in some cases as an alternative to herbicides.

The practicality of this approach has already been demonstrated in experimental field trials, in which the residue of the sorghum plant and sudan grass have been used to provide adequate weed control.

Agricultural scientists will continue to experiment with creative new ways to increase yields, conserve natural resources, and protect the environment. Controlled environment agriculture, hydroponics, new water management technologies,

Aphids and other pests are drawn to the sticky board (above) by its color. The installation, in a greenhouse, is an ecologically sound alternative to insecticides.

new ways to control pests, new techniques for land conservation—advances like these promise to change agricultural practices significantly in the United States. And futurists believe that these technologies are only a foretaste of more spectacular changes to come, including, as we shall see, robotics, weather modification, and space farming, among many other new tools that will become available in future decades.

CHAPTER 7

Making Farms Flourish on Earth—and in Space

For more than a century, futurists have imagined a time when people would live in self-sufficient space colonies with all the comforts of home —along with some not yet dreamed of.

Such a vision has always produced questions about feeding the colonists in space. Will they eat ordinary food? Or will they eat strange new food analogs, chemical substitutes for the foods we know today? And, in either case, where will this food supply come from? *(See Glossary, Food Analogs.)*

In earlier decades, no one could begin to answer these basic questions with any claim to practical knowledge. On the one hand, there had been no exploration of space, no experience of actual conditions there. On the other hand, agricultural practices and people's diets had essentially changed very little since ancient times. Farming basically continued to be technologically primitive. It was based on using up resources that seemed limitless. There seemed to be no way to translate earthly farming into farming in space, where there were very few resources. Now, with the vast changes that are sweeping over agricultural technology, there is the promise not only of revolutionary advances in farming on this planet, but of an eminently practical program for farming in space.

Among the groups that have given serious consideration to farming in space is the National Aeronautics and Space Administration (NASA). Early in 1975 the agency became interested in the work of Gerard K. O'Neill, a professor of physics at Princeton University, whose speculations on space colonies were stirring great interest in the academic community.

In the summer of 1975, NASA sponsored a ten-week project at the Ames Research Center, near Palo Alto, California, whose goal was to "design a system for the colonization of space."

Different colors identify specific crops in this color-enhanced photograph of California farmland taken by an orbiting Landsat satellite.

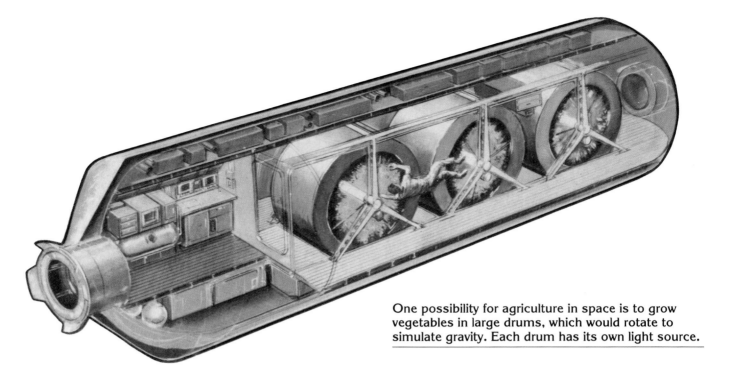

One possibility for agriculture in space is to grow vegetables in large drums, which would rotate to simulate gravity. Each drum has its own light source.

O'Neill was among the team of engineers, chemists, geologists, biologists, and physicists who gathered at Palo Alto. The scientists brought with them a vast amount of existing research on everything from space transport and lunar resources to human nutritional needs and the metabolism of fish. By the end of the summer they had woven all this information into the first detailed, scientific plan for a space community.

A Space Colony Farm

The colony they proposed was a solar-powered artificial planet, shaped like a bicycle wheel and about one mile in diameter. People would live and work inside the four-mile-long "bicycle tube," which would have a comfortable atmosphere and earthlike gravity. Certain low-gravity operations, such as docking, would take place at the hub. Ten thousand people would live in the colony, which would have a closed-loop system allowing water, air, wastes, and other resources to be reused indefinitely.

The report concluded with a description of what visitors might see on a tour of the man-made colony. At a stop for lunch in one of the community dining rooms, they are served a surprisingly down-to-earth meal of chicken, peas, and rice, followed by apple pie—all prepared from crops and animals supplied by the colony's farms. "Hardly the fare that science-fiction writers led you to expect," comments the guide. The visitors then tour one of the colony's three agricultural areas. Its controlled climate is perfectly suited to high-productivity farming all year round. "A couple of minutes' walk brings a view of tiers of fields and ponds and cas-

cading water," says the guide. "The upper level, where you enter, is surrounded by a number of ponds holding about ninety thousand fish. There are similar ponds in the other two farms. From the ponds the water flows down to lower levels where it irrigates fields of corn, sorghum, soybeans, rice, alfalfa, and vegetables and provides water for livestock." Each of the three agricultural areas in the colony grows essentially the same crops. Harvests are staggered to provide a continuous supply.

Farm animals are raised on one of the lower levels. Each farm raises some twenty thousand chickens, ten thousand rabbits, five hundred cattle. They provide eggs, milk, butter, cheese, and meat for the colonists.

The lowest level of the agricultural area is enclosed. Here humidity is kept at a very low level to permit rapid drying of the crops. This speeds up the period between harvesting and the time the food is eaten. Because of its high productivity, the colony's agriculture feeds ten thousand people on the produce of 61 hectares (151 acres).

These seeming miracles are based on sound scientific planning. The crops would be grown in a foot-deep layer of lightweight, nonorganic lunar "soil," obtained as an inexpensive byproduct of mining the moon's abundant mineral resources. The lunar material is made into a growing medium that is rather like vermiculite, a mineral substance used in CEA farming.

The study predicts that the per-acre productivity of the space farms will be high. Yields will be at least ten times those of the average American farm in the 1970s. There are several reasons for this. First, the growing season is continuous and year round, with twenty-four hours of sun each day. Second, carbon dioxide, water, plant nutrition, and temperature levels are controlled precisely to suit the needs of each plant. And finally, the environment is protected from all the harmful influences that regularly affect productivity on earth. Wind, hail, and air pollution do not exist. Weeds, pests, and diseases are controlled by quarantining suspect plants and animals.

In estimating the productivity a space farm could achieve, the NASA team considered reports of the successful use of techniques such as intercropping (see Chapter 2) to increase productivity in densely populated, land-poor regions. They decided that such techniques could be applied to systems of intensive farming in space.

The space colony planners also weighed the pros and cons of a vegetarian diet. They decided that most people eat meat and would miss it; therefore the colony should raise animals. They concluded that this would be economically sound as long as varieties of high-productivity animals were chosen. Beef would have to be a rare treat because cattle are notably poor converters of feed to protein. In fact, they eat about one hundred pounds of feed for every nine pounds of meat they produce. Pigs, chickens, turkeys, and rabbits, on the other hand, could be raised in abundance. Goats produce about twice as much milk as cows so they would supply most dairy products.

In the opinion of at least one space planner, fish will probably be a major food in space, and it may be raised in a highly unusual way. In his book *Colonies in Space,* Thomas Heppenheimer, a member of the NASA scientific team and an aerospace engineer, proposes that fish be raised in specially designed zero-gravity waterless chambers.

"On earth, when a fish is taken from water, gravity makes its gills collapse so that it cannot get oxygen," Heppenheimer says. "In weightless space these same fish might easily 'swim' through an atmosphere of 100 percent humidity, keeping comfortably moist; hydroponic fish, if you will." So as not to waste space in the colony, Heppenheimer would use the acreage beneath the flying fish for some other activity involving weightlessness.

The report ends with the opinion that a tenfold increase in productivity is actually a very conservative estimate. Controlled-environment installations on earth have already achieved large increases in productivity. Crop growing in space

The wheel-like space colony above, nearly a mile wide, could house as many as ten thousand people and be totally self-sufficient in terms of food.

OVERLEAF: In the agricultural area of the space colony, water from the fish ponds on the upper tier (left) would flow down to irrigate crops on the second level and eventually to water livestock on the lowest tier. Crops would be harvested by robot machinery, and a solar-powered train would collect the harvested vegetables and grains. A special control zone for tomatoes is shown at upper right, while at lower right crops dry beneath glass-roofed structures. Continuous sunlight and the controlled environment would result in yields forty times greater than on earth.

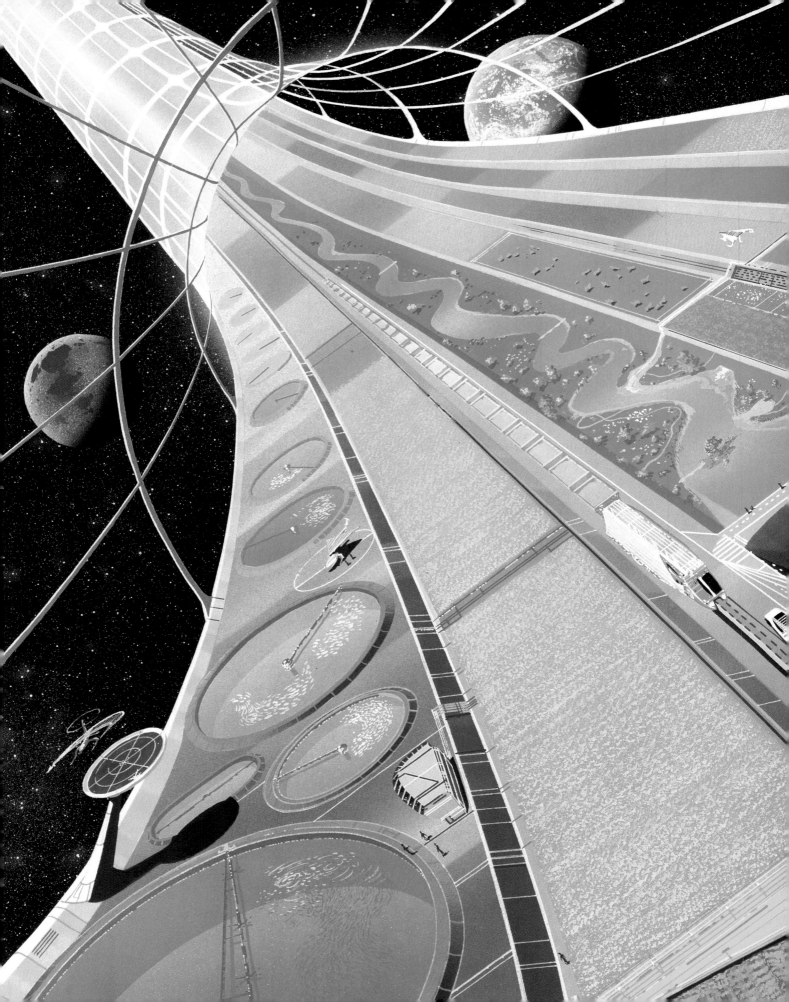

offers even greater advantages. The scientists suggest that increases in some crops, such as corn, may be closer to forty times the levels on earth.

The Rise of Space Agriculture

Since 1975, when the meeting at the Ames Research Center took place, NASA's space planners have focused more closely on exactly how the colonizing of space should proceed. Based on their current planning, smaller space bases will precede the establishment of a large-scale space colony housing thousands of people sometime in the twenty-first century.

Pointing toward that goal, NASA has been authorized to establish a space station in the next ten years. It will permit eight to twelve astronauts to live and work in low earth orbit for periods of up to six months at a time. The next steps will be to set up a base on the moon and then to send off a manned mission to Mars. This mission would culminate in the founding of settlements on Mars.

A common factor running through these exciting future prospects is the need for food. To begin with, the space station will be used to develop the technology needed to provide effective closed life support systems, including the full recycling of air, water, and waste. This would form the technical foundation for the rise of agriculture in space. In fact, current studies have attempted to pinpoint when food grown in space becomes preferable to the use of either stored food or food produced by chemical synthesis. This point occurs, space planners estimate, at about the ten thousand person-day level—a level reached when one hundred astronauts live in space for one hundred days, or ten astronauts live in space for one thousand days.

In time, the space station's population will reach one hundred permanent residents. Plants grown in special artificial-gravity modules will then be used to help revitalize the air and to provide dietary relief from the boredom of "packaged" meals.

American astronauts will return to the moon, possibly before the end of this century, as explorers searching for mineral resources to support space industries and as scientists studying space phenomena. They will also be space farmers, growing food in specially designed facilities.

Looking farther ahead, space planners are now studying the technical tools necessary to support a manned mission to Mars. Perhaps by the year 2010, a spacecraft under nuclear-electric propulsion and carrying a crew of five will depart on a two-and-a-half year journey of exploration to the "red planet." Such a momentous undertaking will eventually be followed by the arrival of the first permanent Martian settlers and the beginning of extraterrestrial agriculture on Mars.

Using Martian water, specially designed agricultural facilities will make portions of the planet bloom. These Martian farms will help to revitalize precious air and water supplies. They will also of course feed the settlers and lay the foundation for the large-scale transformation of the planet. Some aerospace visionaries now contemplate using genetically engineered plants to help tame the harsh Martian climate and to convert the thin Martian atmosphere (95 percent carbon dioxide by volume) into a more moderate earthlike environment. This large-scale modification of an entire planet has been called "planetary engineering" or "terra forming."

Other benefits will flow from the rise of space agriculture. One of the most interesting properties of outer space is that it provides complete biological isolation from the terrestrial biosphere. Geneticists and agricultural scientists working on the space station could conduct genetic engineering experiments considered too hazardous to be performed on earth. Taking advantage of unique conditions in space facilities, such as variable levels of gravity, these scientists might produce varieties of "superplants," which would be of use to both space and terrestrial farmers.

As exciting as the prospect of growing food in space may be, agricultural scientists are well aware that the development of space agriculture cannot be regarded as a panacea for the problems we face on earth.

The NASA team at the Ames Research Center pointed out, "The colonization of space must not detract from efforts to conserve terrestrial resources and improve the quality of life on earth." In the realm of agriculture, these efforts show considerable promise.

Let us now look briefly at some of the scientific and technological developments that seem sure to have an important effect on earthbound agricultural practices in future years.

Satellite Help for Farmers

The first is remote sensing by satellite, which surveys the ever-changing surface of the earth. It has been developing as an important tool of high-technology agriculture since 1974. In that year, the USDA joined with NASA and the National Oceanic and Atmospheric Administration in designing the Landsat system. The first Landsat spacecraft was launched in 1972, and these "eyes in the sky" have become more and more advanced and sensitive. *(See Glossary, Landsat.)*

Landsats do not gather data by cameras. Instead, they use a multispectral scanning device that senses different bands of electromagnetic radiation which are reflected from the earth's surface.

Crops have been found to have their own characteristic capacities to reflect light in the form of electromagnetic radiation. Plants reflect light according to their species, vigor, stage of maturity, and whether or not they are diseased or affected by drought or other kind of stress.

The orbiting antenna system below is a proposed earth observation spacecraft of the future that could monitor earth resources and weather conditions.

Similarly, different soil types and different levels of moisture in the soil also register uniquely on the spectral scanning device. This means that the information gathered by satellite sensors can be used to monitor conditions useful to farmers.

Landsat 5, the most advanced satellite now in use, is about ten feet in length, weighs around twenty-five hundred pounds, and orbits the earth fourteen times a day. Its orbit and field of view are designed so that any given location is observed every fourteen days and always at the same local daylight time.

Landsat 5 transmits its measurements of electromagnetic radiation to ground receiving stations on earth 570 miles below. They arrive line by line, as a series of numerical values, much like a television signal. Computers then convert this digital information into composite images that look like photographs. Each image covers about thirteen thousand square miles.

Remote sensing for agriculture is still in the early stages of its development. The satellite itself is advanced, and the digital data coming back to earth are very detailed. But Landsat's interpreters must still gain experience in relating the information they receive to actual conditions, or what they call "ground truth." This experience will come only when researchers in the field have been able to coordinate enough of their findings with the satellite's findings to develop standard mathematical models. Because of the importance of wheat in world trade, the first intensive studies are being devoted to wheat yields. As time goes on, remote sensing will be able to gather vital data on all economically important crops.

One thing remote sensing data is likely to be used for is estimating world crop production. It is already possible to identify specific crops using Landsat and to measure their acreage with almost 97 percent accuracy. It is also rapidly becoming possible to forecast crop yields at harvest time. With such information, agricultural forecasters will soon be able to tell American farmers which crops will find the best markets abroad.

Remote sensing will also help farmers in many other ways. Among the expected uses for Landsat are: detecting the spread of particular plant path-

A Bird's-Eye View

Supplementing the day-to-day information that farmers and agronomists gain in the field are a variety of remote survey systems. The oldest is aerial survey by airplanes, which makes it possible to see at fairly close range the extent of acreage devoted to a particular crop, to map terrain, and to identify changes in soil type. A recent refinement of aerial survey is color infrared (CIR) photography, which was developed by NASA. Aerial CIR photography is sensitive to gradations of light reflected from foliage, indicating the health or disease of the trees. The citrus growers of Florida have found this technology particularly applicable to their needs. Aerial photos, such as the one above left, enable a citrus farmer to monitor the vigor of every orange and grapefruit tree in his grove. Those trees that appear in red are in good health. Other colors indicate which trees are dead, dying, or in early stages of distress. The farmer then follows up with ground inspection and treatment where needed.

Another NASA-sponsored aid to farmers is satellite surveys of farm acreage. In the photograph above a U.S. Department of Agriculture agronomist at the Lyndon B. Johnson Space Center in Houston takes a close look at pictures transmitted from space as Landsat 2 and Landsat 3 orbit the earth. These photographs convey data that can be translated into useful information about conditions. The same satellite images may also be used to make computer-generated maps like those seen below left. A USDA statistician is shown at his console, developing information on predicted yields of wheat. By referring to a "history" of soil and climate conditions for a given area—a sequence of images taken over a period of time—and applying it to mathematical models of proven reliability, he is able to make a remarkably accurate prediction of the harvest.

ogens; predicting trouble spots where erosion is a problem; managing water resources; and analyzing the effects of droughts.

"Superbird," a highly useful spinoff of Landsat, may come along in the not too distant future to help the individual farmer in managing the day-to-day affairs of his own land. USDA physicist Ray D. Jackson describes it as a "poor man's satellite." As Jackson sees it, Superbird would be inexpensive enough for a few farmers to launch one together as a joint venture. "Parked" about twenty miles above their land, it would be able to gather data and give advice on demand.

What kind of advice would Superbird provide? In a typical example, a farmer asks it to check on the progress of his wheat acres. Superbird reports back promptly, creating an image of the fields on the farmer's office monitor. In one corner of the screen the farmer sees blotches of spectral red. These are actually thermal hot spots, which indicate some sort of crop stress. Not sure whether the stress is due to lack of moisture, disease, or a low supply of nutrients in the soil, the farmer asks his desk computer to make an assessment. To do this the computer uses data stored in its memory bank, specifying the age of the crop, the amount of rainfall to date, the chemical makeup of fertilizers already applied, and so on.

The computer formulates a recommendation. Perhaps the culprit is a shortage of nitrogen in the soil. The farmer then asks the computer to determine the costs of several different courses of action. To do this, the computer considers such factors as the predicted yield with or without additional nutrients, the current market price for wheat, the price of nitrogen, and so on. With the computer's help, the farmer quickly decides that the best course of action is to add a moderate amount of fertilizer.

The Role of Robots

The computer suggests he wait and do this in conjunction with irrigating the fields. When that time comes, the farmer may not even have to go out to the barn to get the fertilizer. Instead, he will instruct a robot to measure out the right amount and pour it into the irrigation system.

Artist Robert McCall envisions a solar farm of the future in Arizona, above. A carpet of solar-sensitive material rises some fifteen feet above the desert,

generating electricity for the farm. Under the carpet,
on the surface of the desert, crops are grown.
Dirigibles float above the farm, unloading cargo.

If the predictions of futurists are correct, "intelligent" machines like this will be common labor-saving devices. Even today, the newest robots are moving beyond the "dumb" machines that must be guided by skilled workers. Smart robots are already being used as fruit pickers by the Israeli citrus industry. The robots have mobile arms equipped with a crude form of "vision." By means of their sensitivity to color, the arms detect fruits that are ripe, then pick them, one by one. Similarly, the Japanese have developed a driverless combine that can harvest wheat or rice while the farmer is miles away.

Even something as difficult as shearing sheep can be done by robots. According to Stewart Key of the University of Western Australia, a shortage of human labor has recently led engineers to design a computer-directed shearing machine. It can shear 88 percent of the wool from a sheep in fifteen minutes, without making a single nick. (Human shearers take only three to four minutes. But they cut the sheep as many as twenty-five times—and they suffer from back problems.)

The Effects of Weather and Climate

The future of open-field farming will also be strongly affected by the weather. The effect of weather—wind, humidity, rainfall, sunshine—on plant growth has been recognized since the beginning of farming. Down to our own time, farmers have done their best to influence favorably the whims and patterns of nature. To change "bad" weather or continue "good" weather, they have tried everything from offerings to the gods to cannon shots and cloud-seeding. Seeding rain clouds with silver iodide may, in fact, cause rain to fall in an area. And using smudge pots to produce heat can protect citrus groves from minor frosts. But neither these nor other techniques have any real effect on the overall climate. In the end, all weather is a response to the sun.

Yet there is some evidence that the earth's climate is changing. What is causing the change and what the lasting effect will be is difficult for scientists to say. But many scientists believe that the changes are man-made, although unintentional. They cite air pollution as one possible cause.

Among its many harmful effects, air pollution can reduce the intensity of sunlight reaching the earth and can change local patterns of rainfall.

Desertification—the erosion of grasslands into desert—is another environmental change that affects the weather. Desertification is the result of overgrazing in an area with a dry climate. Herds of animals simply eat up the ground cover faster than nature can replenish it. This leads to severe erosion and drought. As the natural ecosphere is altered, a change in climate follows. The Sahara Desert in North Africa and the Thar Desert in India are steadily being enlarged in this way.

Some environmentalists are also concerned about the "greenhouse effect," a rise in the level of carbon dioxide in the atmosphere that could result in a rise in the world's temperature. Scientists believe that the increase in carbon dioxide has two causes. One is the burning of large amounts of fossil fuels—coal, petroleum, and natural gas. Another is the destruction of the world's forests. Plants absorb carbon dioxide and produce oxygen. Cutting down forests reduces the conversion of carbon dioxide to oxygen. Some scientists have estimated that the amount of carbon dioxide present in the atmosphere could double by the year 2030.

How does an increase in carbon dioxide affect temperature? Carbon dioxide reflects heat back down on the earth's surface. When the level of carbon dioxide increases, the amount of heat reflected also increases.

A rise in temperature worldwide of as much as 3 degrees Centigrade on average has been predicted, and it could have dramatic effects, melting polar ice caps and raising sea levels. Millions of acres of coastal farmlands could be covered by water. Heat and moisture levels in inland farming regions could also be altered.

Such changes would have an enormous impact on agriculture. The U.S. grain belt, for instance, might lose its primacy in corn and wheat production and become semiarid rangeland. It would enjoy warmer temperatures and would also have increased levels of carbon dioxide, which would be helpful to photosynthesis and thus speed plant growth.

Halophytes, crops that can grow in saltwater or salty soil, are expected to play a major role in feeding the world's growing population. Above, halophytes are farmed in Puerto Penasco, Mexico.

A number of circumstances could modify the effects of the carbon dioxide buildup, however. For this reason scientists are not sure if there is really a warming trend and, if so, how serious it will be. Robert H. Shaw of Iowa State University, a leading figure in agricultural climatology, believes that "wiggles" in the climate, not trends, will be of most concern in the immediate future. The "wiggles" he refers to are sudden shifts and changes in weather patterns in relatively small areas of the world. They may be short cycles of drought, extremely cold winters, summers with record high temperatures, and shifts in the jet stream and in the ocean currents such as occurred in 1982–83 with the Pacific current called "El Niño." Changes such as these can produce crisis conditions in regional agriculture, causing major crop losses for thousands of farmers and food shortages for millions of people. Shaw and other experts do not know whether these shifts have been caused by a permanent change in climate or whether they are simply the result of a temporary movement in an unstable system of climate.

In any event, Shaw is one of many climatologists who believe that long-term agricultural policy should include preparations for future adverse shifts in climate. Among the preparations he advocates are: programs to encourage the wider use of land for agriculture, including land now considered to be marginal for farming; the storage of substantial amounts of grain; and further research into ways to modify climate.

Meanwhile, farmers are benefitting from more and more accurate government weather forecasting services. Once there were only the predictions of the Farmers' Almanac and local wisdom to guide the farmer. Now farmers are helped by both short-range and long-range forecasts based on the constant monitoring of ground stations and weather satellites. Still more accurate long-range predictions are expected in the future, fostered by the growth of a worldwide network of cooperating meteorological centers. By international agreement, each country that participates in this network will gather data on sixteen factors that influence climate. These range from solar radiation to surface wind and soil temperatures. The information will be used to predict weather months and even years ahead.

How Diets May Change

With so many sweeping changes already altering agricultural practices, and so many more promised, it should not be surprising that futurists expect our diet to change, too. Dietary changes will probably occur more slowly in some parts of the world than in others. Generally, the greatest resistance to changes in dietary patterns will come from people's desire to continue eating their customary foods.

There will probably be little resistance to new foods on the grounds that they do not supply adequate nutrition. Scientists have already proven that they can synthesize tasty imitations of milk, cheese, meat, seafood, and starches.

Among the major changes to look for are a number of cheaper sources of protein derived from various plants. Soybeans are already found as fillers in many processed foods. They will almost certainly become more important in the American diet as ways are found to improve their flavor and texture. Because Americans are so fond of eating meat, many of the vegetable proteins will probably be made into meat analogs (chemical substitutes). Cheap cuts of meat will be added in the final stages of processing for flavor and color. Cottonseed, sunflower seeds, rapeseeds, and some yet-to-be-discovered plants (see "Supermarket on a Stalk," page 64) will also become important new sources of protein.

In addition, futurists envision more exotic sources for the production of protein. Leaves, grasses, and waterweeds may be processed into tasty "leaf protein concentrates," or LPCs. Deepwater ocean fish now thrown away when caught will be made into fish protein concentrates (FPC) once scientists find ways to make them smell and taste better. Bacteria, yeasts, fungi, and algae are other possible sources of single-cell protein (SCP) that are being investigated. One example is the blue-green algae called *Spirulina maxima*, a one-celled plant without roots, a stem, or leaves. Spirulina has been eaten since ancient times by people living around Lake Chad in Africa. The Mayas of ancient Mexico also ate it. Spirulina is currently being grown commercially in California's Imperial Valley. The algae, bred in ponds the size of football fields, have been described as the ideal crop. Raised under controlled conditions, spirulina algae double themselves every five days.

Spirulina has an average of 65 percent protein. At present, it is eaten chiefly as a nutritional supplement by athletes and vegetarians. But it could probably be made into all sorts of foods. Perhaps its most promising use is as a dietary supplement in poor nations where protein sources are desperately needed.

A Time of Plenty

Cheap alternatives to traditional foods may become a reality in the near future. Will this make farms and farmers obsolete? Will roast turkey, cranberries, and pumpkin pie be driven from the Thanksgiving table by machine-made look-alikes? Probably not. For the foreseeable future, alternative foods will be used mainly to alleviate starvation in famine situations and in the less developed areas of the world. Most futurists believe that wherever the climate, soil, and technology are favorable (as they have been in the United States), traditional foods will be grown and they will continue to be our principal source of food and nutrition.

At the same time, as this book has made abundantly clear, farms and farmers of the future will certainly be more efficient, producing increased quantities of better-grown crops on less land. And they will do this with less waste of precious nonrenewable resources.

Visitors to The Land exhibit at EPCOT Center see some of the ways that science and technology will make this possible. Others will be developed. But it will be the responsibility of the peoples and nations of the world to make the wisest use of the newest and most innovative agricultural ideas. If they do, the future will be a time of plenty, with the people of the earth sharing in the bounty of the land and sharing, too, in the "creative partnership with nature" that should be our goal.

Robots tend crops that grow on floating platforms around a sea city of the future. Water from the ocean would evaporate, rise to the base of the platforms (leaving the salt behind), and feed the crops.

Glossary

Allelopathy The capacity of certain plants to release into the soil chemicals that are poisonous to other plants.

Aquaculture Raising fish and other aquatic creatures under controlled conditions—in short, fish farming.

Cloning Creating duplicates of plants that are genetically identical. This may be accomplished through sexless reproduction, including the development of an organism from a single cell. Cloning may also be used to create duplicate individual genes.

Closed-System Farming Farming in which a variety of crops are grown on a relatively small farm. Each crop is scientifically selected to be environmentally beneficial and to contribute to the farm's overall needs.

Conservation Tillage Techniques for preparing the soil to raise crops that have been developed to avoid soil erosion and depletion.

Controlled Environment Agriculture (CEA) The general term used for the raising of crops in large greenhouses or in other sheltered environments where conditions such as light and temperature are controlled to produce the best possible growth.

Crossbreeding Mating parent plants that have one or more outstanding characteristics, such as size or color, in the hope that these characteristics will be combined and passed on to the offspring.

DNA or Deoxyribonculeic Acid A substance found in the nuclei of cells of all living organisms. It is the principal constituent of chromosomes, the structure that transmits hereditary characteristics from one generation to the next. Chromosomes contain genes, the ultimate units that determine hereditary characteristics *(see Gene Splicing)*.

Erosion The wearing away of the earth's surface by natural forces such as wind, water, and glaciers. Erosion washes away topsoil, and some farming methods, such as removing plant cover and trees, hasten this process.

Food Analogs Artificial food substitutes. In the future, they may be produced by using the chemicals from inedible materials.

Gene Splicing A technique used to transplant a gene or genes from one species of plant or animal to another. The genes that are transplanted are contained in portions of molecules of DNA. Using this technique, characteristics associated with the gene can be passed on artificially *(see DNA)*.

Herbicides Substances used to destroy plants. Those used in farming are designed to kill weeds and leave crops unharmed.

Hybrid The offspring of a plant or animal that results from the crossbreeding of two different varieties or species of parents.

Hydroponics Growing plants in water that is enriched with necessary nutrients.

Integrated Pest Management (IPM) A system of controlling rather than eliminating plant pests, such as insects, weeds, and pathogens, through a combination of biological, physical, and chemical controls *(see Pathogen)*.

Intercropping A technique for growing two or more crops side by side in alternating rows. This technique can result in improved soil fertility and increased crop yields *(see Multiple Cropping)*.

Landsat A satellite that surveys the surface of the earth. Its scanning device senses different bands of electromagnetic radiation reflected from the physical features and vegetation on the earth's surface. The information it collects can be used to monitor farming conditions such as erosion and crop growth.

Monoculture Farming in which just one kind of crop, such as wheat, is grown on a large scale.

Multiple Cropping A technique for choosing the best plants for intercropping so that crop growth and soil chemistry are benefited.

Pathogen A specific organism that causes a disease, such as a bacterium, virus, or fungus.

Photosynthesis The process by which plants make food. Plant cells containing chlorophyll convert sunlight into energy and use it to combine carbon dioxide in the air with water in the soil to produce starches, sugars, and proteins.

Plant Growth Regulators Artificially produced chemical equivalents of the natural substances called hormones. Growth regulators are used to produce more desirable performance in a plant, for instance, to make crops bigger or faster or ripen all at once.

Soilless Farming Farming in which crops are grown in water or some other medium instead of soil. Such farming is usually done indoors under controlled conditions.

Symbiosis The usually beneficial relationship of two or more different organisms in close association.

Tissue Culture The technique of producing plants with desired characteristics by changing one plant's genetic makeup. The change is accomplished by growing tissue cells in the laboratory under special conditions. Through this technique, scientists can, for example, produce plants adapted to salty soil or to very hot temperatures.

Index

Boldface numbers indicate illustrations.